the Art & Craft of
STORY
2nd Practitioner's Manual

the ART & CRAFT OF STORY

2ND PRACTITIONER'S MANUAL

VICTORIA MIXON

Mendocino, California

Copyright © 2011 by Victoria Mixon

All rights reserved. No part of this book may be reproduced in any form or by any electronic or mechanical means including information storage and retrieval systems, without permission in writing from the author.

victoriamixon.com

Published by La Favorita Press
PO Box 1203, Mendocino, CA 95460
lafavoritapress.com

ISBN 978-0-9845427-3-4
Library of Congress Control Number: 2011939022

Text set in Book Antiqua, by Monotype Staff, Microsoft Typography. Titles and headings set in Poor Richard, by Keystone Type Foundry.

The Art & Craft of Story™, La Favorita Press™ and the La Favorita graphic are trademarks of La Favorita Press. All other trademarks are trademarks of their respective owners.

Manufactured in the United States of America

Acknowledgements

Again—I am so deeply grateful to all my editing clients and blog and magazine/laboratory readers, particularly Kathryn and Sita and students Miles and Peter, who surreptitiously contributed to the book. When I need someone to write to and for, you are there. I'm very grateful to Lucia Orth for her kind and meticulous help and to Jon Green for wonderful conversation. And I am of course eternally grateful to my husband, Jeff Osier-Mixon, who does everything around here except write my books for me, and my son, Haven, who is the light of my life and the joy of my heart, the real motivation behind everything I do.

Table of Contents

INTRODUCTION

The State of the Industry 15

PART 1: STORYTELLING

Chapter 1: Loving in the Time of Cholera
with Gabriel Garcia Marquez 21

Chapter 2: Searching for Entertainment-Industry Intelligence
.... 25

Chapter 3: How Stories are Written 29

    Accepting the Gullibility of Being a Writer 29
    Reviewing the Definition of a Story 30
    Reviewing the Definition of Fiction 35
    Reviewing the Purpose of Storytelling 37

Chapter 4: Character Arc/Narrative Arc 39

Chapter 5: Graphing in Three Dimensions 45

Chapter 6: The Only Two Stories 47

    Mining Yourself 47
    Differentiating Between Together & Alone 50
    Molding & Being Molded By Relationship 53
    Aiming Past Ecstasy through Quest 57

Chapter 7: Reading with Attention 61

    Reading for Plot Design 61
    Reading for Character Development 64

Table of Contents

Chapter 8: Creating Reader Addiction 67

    Creating the Basic Tension in Character 67
    Creating the Basic Tension in Plot 71

Chapter 9: Creating Reader Fulfillment 75

    Touching Your Reader's Core with Resonance 75
    Playing Fair with Resonance 79

Chapter 10: Drawing an Analogy 83

    Drawing a Logo 83
    Applying the Analogy to Storytelling 86

CHARACTER IS *CONTENT*

Chapter 11: Being Mesmerized with Louisa May Alcott 93

Chapter 12: Hunting the Ghost Tiger 97

    Taking the Tiger by the Tail 97
    Focusing the Tiger 102

Chapter 13: Developing Character 107

    Differentiating Yourself from Your Reader 107
    Seeing What Your Reader Sees in Character 109
    Understanding Sympathetic Character 113

Chapter 14: Condensing & Contrasting Characters 119

    Condensing Multiple Characters into One 119
    Condensing Characters for Internal Conflict 121
    Condensing Characters for Contrast 123

Chapter 15: Using Character 129

    Using Character to Create Plot 129
    Using Character to Fuel Momentum 132
    Using Character to Addict Your Reader 137

Chapter 16: Layering Character 141

    Layering Character with Behavior 142
    Layering Character with Confusion 143
    Layering Character with Two Classical Needs 144

PLOT IS CONTEXT

Chapter 17: Designing an Impossible Plot
with Maria Dermout..149

Chapter 18: Beating Your Drum 153

Chapter 19: Designing a Crescendo 159

 Fatal Ignition 163
 Backstory 165
 Three Acts..168
 Two Plot Points 172
 One Fulcrum 177
 Feinting..181
 The Whole Point 185

Chapter 20: Hook 187

 Act I: Hook 188
 Act I: Hook climax — *Fatal Ignition*....................192
 Act I: Backstory 195
 Act I: Conflict #1 196
 Act I: Conflict #1 climax — *First Plot Point*........199

Chapter 21: Development 203

 Act II: Conflict #2..203
 Act II: Conflict #2 climax — *Fulcrum* 208
 Act II: Conflict #3..211
 Act II: Conflict #3 climax — *Second Plot Point*..215

Chapter 22: Climax 219

 Act III: Faux Resolution......................................219
 Act III: Faux Resolution climax — *Feinting* 223
 Act III: Climax 226
 Act III: Climax climax — *the Whole Point*..........230

Chapter 23: More Climax 235

 Pin-Pointing Your Climax..................................235
 Making a Scene Out of Your Climax.................237
 Structuring Your Climax....................................242
 Building Total, Complex, Shocking, & Inevitable
  Significance into Your Climax...........................244

Table of Contents

Chapter 24: Layering Plot 249
    Main plotline..250
    Subplots...250
    Plot threads 253
Chapter 25: Epiphany..257

PART 2: REVISION

Chapter 26: Writing & Rewriting with Franz Kafka...............263
Chapter 27: Vision & Revision..267
    Rethinking Motivation for Character Arc 267
    Reorganizing Events for Narrative Arc................................274
    Re-igniting Theme through Tao..279
Chapter 28: Reshuffling Your Deck 281
    Brainstorming...281
    Overall Organization 282
    Scene-by-Scene Arc 283
    Intuition..284
    Fun..285
    Staying in Motion 286
    Resting When Necessary 286
    Rewriting Out of Chronology 286
    Taking Notes...287
    A Word of Warning about Resolution........................287
Chapter 29: Spiraling Up the Helix..289
    First Draft..289
    Second Draft 290
    Third Draft..291
    Nth Draft...292
    Final Draft...294
Chapter 30: Going Beyond the Beyond 297

xii

Conclusion

Riding Out the Winter of Our Discontent 301
Index 305

Introduction

The State of the Industry
Fiction

One day last year some of us were talking about work habits—whether or not it's essential to write every single day, how to prioritize writing projects, whether or not to quantify output or time, what's the best way to start writing every day.

And the answers all came down to one thing:

Why are we writing our stories?

Maybe we're writing them because we grew up in the 1950s and sixties and seventies reading books by authors who—even though they weren't famous—still made a sort of lower-middle-class living staying home with a typewriter all day doing what they were good at and they loved. And that was the future we saw for ourselves. Because we just loved books.

Or maybe we're writing because, even though we've never been writers, these stories came to us, and we really, seriously, passionately wanted to tell them, but the more we work on them the more we want to tell them *exactly right*. And so we're struggling to learn how to discover exactly the right way.

Or maybe we're writing to become the next J.K. Rowling and make history in the industry and become famous as that break-out success everyone's still talking about twenty years later. Truth be told, when we think this way we probably aren't thinking about twenty years from now. We're probably only thinking about next year and whether or not we'll be so excited we'll vomit on Oprah.

Or maybe we're writing because everywhere we go these days people are asking us if we're on Twitter and Facebook, whether or not we have blogs, if we're 'online,' and when we *do* go online everywhere we look people are talking about how we have to start marketing our books before we even write them, and they're critiquing each other's manuscripts and offering for critique their own manuscripts on forums, and they're bemoaning their wordcounts and trading tips on blogging agents and asking us if we're doing NaNoWriMo this year.

And as soon as we ask ourselves, "Am I? Why not?" we realize we've opened the Pandora's Box of writing advice that hammers at us relentlessly from all directions, "Build your platform! Drive your traffic! Leverage your social media network! Accumulate your subscribers!" As though the whole world were out there right this second waiting around just for *us*—for us to give it what *it wants*—and none too patiently either. And we're thinking, *Huh. I always thought I was supposed to learn how to write well before I could sell anything I'd written. How wrong* was I?. . .

Now, more than ever in history, the aspiring writer must guard against other people's agendas. We must consider every day with as much clarity and self-awareness as we can muster why we, personally, write. We must ask ourselves why we write *what* we write, just what we want to get out of writing, and how badly we want to get it. We must ask every single time we sit down with our stories, "Why this? Why me? Why now?"

We must keep our heads when all those around us are losing theirs.

Because the world of illusion has finally come off the page and taken over the actual experience of being a writer. It can seem it's no longer about getting into that page and sinking with luxurious, tactile pleasure through the layers and layers and layers of brilliant and significant and riveting detail to the core underlying everything we could ever hope to write. As though it's no longer about climbing back out of those depths when we look up and around and realize we're sitting in a chair, at a desk, in a room, and our lives are in here with us. No longer about going downstairs to sit on the front steps in the twilight after a solid day's work and think of those satisfying pages, smell the grass, listen to the birds, watch the clouds cross the iridescent sky, feel the good, firm earth beneath our bare feet.

It's all Barnum & Bailey, now, lost in the virtual blogosphere twenty-four hours a day, seven days a week, always and forever unto infinity.

We must remember, as we live our lives—this life of the writer in the twenty-first century—what an illusion the circus is. And remember what they say is born every minute.

We didn't choose this craft to be the craft of our souls just so we could be *that*.

We must turn our backs on the circus.

We must turn to our stories.

Part 1
Storytelling

Chapter 1

Loving in the Time of Cholera with Gabriel Garcia Marquez

Storytelling for the ages

I have a wonderful writer friend whom I love to death, but he has dyslexia like nobody's business, plus he doesn't think of himself as an intellectual. He's great if one of you has to climb a drainpipe to break into an upstairs apartment in the middle of a blistering hot summer afternoon. *Ask me how I know.* (He said, "Grab my keys." He did *not* say, "Don't grab one of those extra sets of car keys my roommate leaves lying around everywhere in plain sight.")

And he's actually quite an imaginative writer, because his dyslexia forces him to be certain every single word he puts down he really *needs* to put down. Years ago, when we were young and intense and tragically-hip, I used to type his poetry for him. He'd lean over my shoulder in his ratty San Francisco apartment on lower Haight Street (where the dealers and druggies were even worse than in my neighborhood in the upper Tenderloin), watching me disentangle 'cigarette' from the extra y's and z's that he'd given it and laughing. "So *that's* how you spell that!"

But it took him two years to read Gabriel Garcia Marquez' *One Hundred Years of Solitude,* carrying it everywhere with him all day long every day. By the time he was done, it was as though he'd won the Olympics. I seriously thought it might take him. . .one hundred years. . .of solitude. . .

Because there's only one thing that's going to inspire a severely dyslexic non-intellectual to get all the way through *One Hundred Years of Solitude.*

And that's stunning craft.

Marquez is a craftsperson of infinitely fine sensibility. We could talk for hours (maybe I will) about how he gets away with writing entire 400-page novels of one paragraph about characters all with the same name. It's a miracle.

But where he really clobbers us with his talent is in his endings.

Do you know why *Love in the Time of Cholera* is named that?

Because the final scene could only be orchestrated 1) between people in love, and 2) during a time of cholera.

Or what about Mario Vargas Llosa's *Aunt Julia and the Scriptwriter*? What kind of madman comes up with a love story that revolves around a 1950s radio soap opera producer (*not* one of the lovers) whose single marketing mechanism is personally insulting a random handful of people? Complete with a rat eating something nobody should ever talk about a rat eating? I read that book as a very young adult and was blown backward against the wall by the manic glee of Llosa's literary *chutzpah.*

If we can learn anything from these pillars of twentieth-century South American literature, it is that storytelling is (or was recently, anyway) alive and thriving in parts of the world with low literacy rates.

Why do you suppose that is?

Now I'm going to do something unpopular, and that is take a swipe at Khaled Hosseini's *The Kite Runner*.

The Kite Runner had me completely engrossed for fully half the novel. It was gripping, it was detailed, it was powerful, it was real. The protagonist walks a fine line between wealthy Afghani political power and poor oppressed masses. Sometimes he stays on it. Sometimes he falls off. The details of his struggle are beautiful, harsh, and believable. He's *human*.

Then he and his father finally make it to the U.S. I always start to lose interest when characters with fascinatingly different experiences wind up living boring mainstream American lives, but I was rolling with that, rolling with the exploration of how the loss of their wealth and political power affected them, because up until there it had all been so true.

Then he grows up and goes back.

And this should have been the heart of the novel, everything a Climax is meant to be. We should have gotten to go into this character's childhood culture—which we have some real identification with now, because of that lush first half of the novel—and lived the internal drama of what happens on atmospheric re-entry. What happens when you put a human being through that. What happens to their insides.

Instead, we get a bizarre new plotline about hunting down a child through the evil tyranny of the Taliban and adopting it.

Heh? A new character? This late in the book? Someone we're supposed to bond to and feel enormous investment in? Someone we don't know anything about except second-hand through another character's version of what's happened? Someone so important we're willing to drop the whole exploration of human experience we've been caught up in *up until this point* and suddenly veer off into a completely different

Loving in the Time of Cholera

plot involving the child of a character we *might* feel bonded to based on that lush build-up, except that he's never put in an appearance, and a situation that *might* matter to us if we'd had any idea such a thing could eventually happen?

Suddenly it's all violence and mayhem, the writer telling us what to think and how to feel about the Taliban, a totally different story from the long, meticulous accumulation of character and atmosphere of the earlier part of the book.

Don't do this to yourself. Don't force the awareness of your literary limitations on your reader by ignoring the true story you have chosen to tell.

Read *Love in the Time of Cholera* and study the plot and style. Marquez is very clear from the outset: this is not memoir, this is fiction. Fermina and Florentino spend the entire novel spanning the years of their lives at a distance, their youthful love long lost in the myriad of nuances that make up the profound truth about life lived out over decades. Watch how Marquez builds the plot points with subtle, unerring care. Sink up to your eyeballs in the wonderful plethora of telling detail and characterization, the gradual, sure-handed building of inevitable tension.

Then read the pen-penultimate page about the armed patrol on the river guarding against pestilence.

Three hundred and fifty pages—and the answer to one simple question is where this story was going *all along*.

Chapter 2

Searching for Entertainment-Industry Intelligence

A crash course

My husband and I fell in love under the shadow of SETI.

SETI, in case you don't know, stands for Search for Extra-Terrestrial Intelligence. When one morning sixteen years ago my new boss (and future husband) pointed out that the company we worked for was right down the hall from the SETI offices, I laughed out loud. I didn't know you could rent office space in Silicon Valley from which to search for ET.

But as it happens, SETI, in spite of its *X-Files*-type mission, enjoys a serious reputation among scientists and serves as a funding clearinghouse for a great deal of astronomical research, with enormous grants from some very highly-placed institutions indeed.

All this is by way of explaining where I spent a certain weekend last summer.

My husband had spent the week right before that in Boston leading seminars at one of the major Linux conferences, where he was approached by the SETI people to attend their first annual conference. He was one of a handful of open-source advocates invited to be involved in a discussion on moving

Searching for Entertainment-Industry Intelligence

SETI's software to open source. He was also invited to their black-tie gala, at which astronauts, Star Trek stars, and big names in astronomy got up and talked about the future of space exploration. They were holding this conference at a large hotel in Silicon Valley, only a few hours' drive from where we live. So we went. Of course!

But the really important part of the conference came the day after the black-tie gala, when we attended a talk by the Director of the National Academy of Sciences' Science & Entertainment Exchange on the question: *How can we better bridge the gap between science-fiction entertainment and science?*

We watched a wonderful pastiche of movie clips to illustrate this intriguing question, and afterward the Director of the Science & Entertainment Exchange spoke long and eloquently. She brought up several points that, in my mind, all fit into the puzzle the same way:

- Laypeople learn "science" from sci-fi entertainment
- Using science in sci-fi entertainment *significantly influences* the behavior of 'consumers' (a sitcom featuring science about breast cancer resulted in a major increase in women across the country getting check-ups, a sitcom based on forensic science resulted in a four-fold increase in enrollment in forensic studies programs)
- A fictitious hacker staring at a screen for twenty seconds and yelping, "Eureka!" is a far cry from the real hacker who stares at a screen for weeks on end before unraveling the complexities in their way
- The stories of scientists and their search for information often make gripping telling
- *It's more interesting to know the truth*

She explained that the National Academy of Sciences consults, when asked, on sci-fi movies and TV shows (which is where this Director's job comes in). They also, when not asked to consult, stand by watching the ensuing confusion.

"What can we do about this disconnect?" the Director of the Science & Entertainment Exchange asked.

She described the elitism among scientists that keeps them from being interested in fiction, the lack of understanding among many writers that science-fiction must be based on—who knew?—science. She even told us about her scientist husband's attempt to write a screenplay on what he knows about the potential and lack of potential in time travel, outraged by the ignorance displayed in time-travel sci-fi. ("This is really hard!" he finally said.)

She proposed a Writing Workshop in which writers and scientists would be paired off, so the scientists could keep the writers in the real world while they developed their stories.

Fabulous! I thought, *This all makes perfect sense.*

The truth is that a storyteller is dependent upon the facts of the reality they share with their reader—the hidden life-&-death struggles controlling all human character, the cause-&-effect of events in a temporal world, the meticulous, sensitive selection and accumulation of real details—to create a reflection of life that, when gazed into, resonates with a profundity that's always present in reality but often missed.

Storytelling is not something that interferes with life. It's not about faking or trivializing reality for the sake of the writer. Storytelling is about waking the reader up to the life that's *really there.*

We must look for true aspects of character that we find utterly riveting. Explore real needs that power enormous agendas. Find ways to embed in these riveting characters with these powerful needs the counter-needs that create, deep inside them, internal conflict that rings inside the reader with devastating recognition.

"I *know* this person," the reader thinks. "With all their beauty and horror, their insight and idiocy, their innocence and corruption. *This person is me!*"

Then we give our characters some fascinating premise. What if ionizing the air could bend lightwaves to alter the paths of lasers? (An example of true science from the Director's talk.) What if time machines were possible, but altering the past through time travel were not? (Another example.) What if ghosts were the vibrations of the subatomic 'strings' that once made up the bodies of the living, continuing to reverberate after the bodies are gone? (I made up that one.)

What kind of nightmare could that create?

We put our characters into that nightmare.

And we design a plotline—along the lines of classic structure—around deeper and deeper exploration of the detailed, proven science that not only makes that nightmare possible but contains the *only conceivable antidote.*

We illuminate the eloquent search for truth that drives us all.

Chapter 3

How Stories are Written
An education

Accepting the Gullibility of Being a Writer

Last summer, I started an experiment on my blog. Instead of long, ~~opinionated~~ thoughtful posts on events going on in the publishing industry, I started posting numbered lists. Just silly ways of saying, "Write with your brains, folks."

Wow. My stats doubled the day I started and tripled a couple of days later. And they kept rising after that until they took an exponential leap and I went into blogosphere hyperspeed.

Who would have guessed? *People love lists.*

I was particularly impressed by the response to the first one, in which I claimed to know "107 Things You Should Know About Being a Published Author." Now, I don't know 107 things about being a published author. *Nobody* knows 107 things about being a published author. Even Stephen King doesn't know 107 things about being a published author. But we're willing to believe someone does!

"Hot dog," we're thinking. "The whole instruction manual! I can now plan my life. *Finally.*"

Granted, those of us who are so into such things are writers, not readers. We're just a tiny bit gullible because we're *striving so hard* to get somewhere, not simply looking for a temporary escape. It's our intense need to *become something* that drives us, not our intense need to *stop* being quite so much ourselves for just a while.

Those really are different needs.

Because working in fiction makes us a bit crazy. I know this. You know this. We're concentrating, we're concentrating. We're concentrating on something we want with our whole souls—to be really good writers—until we lose track of little things like perspective and, you know, maybe our native horse sense. It becomes quite easy to believe someone has figured out all 107 things we need to know about what's going to happen to us when we get published, thereby simplifying our lives down to just this part, the part about *creating* something to publish. And that is a huge gift in this day and age, when absolutely everyone and their grandmother is stampeding toward publication, and we're just running along with the herd hoping we don't get trampled under their thousands of little cloven hooves.

Besides, what can writers *not* believe? Our greatest joy is hanging out with imaginary people. We *like* believing things we know for a fact aren't true.

Reviewing the Definition of a Story

So what is the definition of a story?

And who gets to say?

There are a couple of well-known angles on this time-honored question, pointing at it from different directions.

The Art & Craft of Story

First, there's Flannery O'Connor's wonderful discussion in the essays in *Mystery and Manners*—collected from her papers and edited by her friends Robert and Sally Fitzgerald after her death—in which she defines a story as 'a full action with a point.'

Then there's the canonical example:

The king died, and then the queen died. (**plot**)
The king died, and then the queen died of grief. (**story**)

This example illuminates two essential aspects of the difference between plot—an action or series of actions—and story—a *full* action with a *point*.

One essential aspect is causality. **Cause-&-effect**.

And the other essential aspect is **character**. Story is not just plot. Story is plot *plus* character.

Story is based upon cause-&-effect.

And story is based upon character.

Which, if we look at it from the right angle, are almost exactly the same thing.

Plot

King Rupert learns he's dying. However, he has no heir. He tells Queen Isabella he has an illegitimate daughter. He introduces Isabella and Maggie. He dies, and Isabella becomes ruler. Isabella is hit by a bus.

Character

King Rupert is suffering from a terminal disease. This is tragic not only because Rupert is king of a small principality without an heir, but also because Rupert's a darn nice guy who takes good care of his people. The only thing nobody knows is

31

that Rupert has an illegitimate daughter, Maggie, from a liaison with a close friend of adolescence. Oh, yes, and Rupert is deeply, madly in love with his wife, Queen Isabella.

Isabella is a hot-headed but basically good-hearted activist, prone to launching herself into confrontations on a whim without pausing for little things like diplomacy. As much as she helps some of her people, she tends to alienate others, so she definitely does not want Rupert's job, now or ever. Her and Rupert's childlessness is an issue for the kingdom, but in fact means she is not manacled by motherhood as so many women in her position are. What Isabella really wants is to be an adventurer. She sublimates her hunger for excitement in her profound, sincere love for her husband, King Rupert. Right up until the day she gets hit by a bus.

Story

King Rupert learns he's ill and most likely dying. That causes him to re-think his situation regarding his kingdom, his wife, and his illegitimate daughter, Maggie. That causes him to face the possibility that Maggie could cause trouble for Isabella when he dies. *That* causes him to go to Isabella to confess Maggie's existence to her.

Isabella learns Rupert is ill and most likely dying. That causes her to become more hot-headed than normal. That causes her to tangle with embryo-rights activists over stem-cell research. *That* causes her to create a national incident.

Maggie is a medical intern at the kingdom's major medical research facility. She learns King Rupert is ill. That causes her to throw herself into her stem-cell research, staying up night after night without sleep, desperate to find a cure for her country's leader and patron. That causes her to become unstable. That causes her to attend a major embryo-rights demonstration in a less-than-reasonable frame of mind. That causes her to give an impromptu speech. That causes Isabella to use her speech as a rallying point for a passionate—if slightly incoherent—expression of her own anguish. That causes Maggie to mistake Isabella for an embryo-rights spokesperson. And *that* causes Maggie to turn on Isabella, sparking the national incident...

Do you see how we're heading for the last conflict—the scene in which Rupert confesses Maggie's existence to Isabella—loaded for bear?

Character is the basis of all fictional cause-&-effect. Why? Because we read to learn how some folks *will* do. We like human nature! We find it endlessly fascinating. Why *do* people go and do things? Why *don't* we all just stay home twiddling our thumbs?

And—most importantly—when we *don't*, how are we supposed to handle the inevitable crises we bring crashing down upon our own heads?

So we've got this last conflict set up, and we go into it:

Story Climax

Rupert goes to Isabella, who has just come home from causing the national incident and is in her boudoir being cleaned up and first-aided by her ladies, wishing she were in the Himalayas dealing with something reasonable like a nice, quiet avalanche. Rupert sends away the ladies and is about to confess to Maggie's existence.

Meanwhile, Maggie arrives at the castle gates, prepared to take down the queen for interfering with essential stem-cell research that could possibly save the life of the king, but on her way to Isabella's chambers she learns from the servants that

How Stories are Written

Isabella was, in fact, *defending* Maggie's research. This causes her to break down in tears, so when she is finally shown into the queen's and king's presence, she's a stumbling, sobbing wreck.

This causes Rupert to run to her and throw his arms around her.

This causes Maggie and Isabella to go into shock, which gives Rupert a chance to tell them Maggie is his daughter. This causes Isabella and Maggie to be reconciled (faux resolution), but the effort of confession causes Rupert to collapse, and he croaks in their arms.

This causes Isabella, stunned and devastated, her whole life a shambles, to run raving with grief into the street and out into traffic...

...which causes her to be hit by a bus.

Do you see how it is the characters' personalities—their needs and desires—that create the cause-&-effect that fuel the story? If we gave them different personalities, different needs, different desires, the cause-&-effect would be something completely different. And the plot (the king dies, then the queen dies) would be a completely different story.

This is how we can tell basically the same plots over and over again throughout history—there really aren't that many—and yet continue to tell an endless panorama of stories. This is what Honoré de Balzac was attempting with his gazillion hilarious little stories: an infinitely entertaining and touching and educational portrait of *The Human Comedy*.

What would this story have been if Rupert were a lovable psycho? A loser? A mad scientist? A warmonger? Secretly a wizard with power over life and death?

What would it have been if Isabella were a useless wimp? A monster? A madwoman? An exhausted mother? A schemer? A brilliant leader?

What if there had been no Maggie, but a legitimate heir of Rupert and Isabella with their own needs and desires? Or both? If the people were a force pitted against the royalty? If there were yet other forces involved that we haven't even *thought* of?

Why—someone would have to tell that story!

Reviewing the Definition of Fiction

We've started off with the definition of story through *cause-&-effect* based on *character*. As it should be! Now let's review the definition of **fiction**: storytelling through the written word.

One day last year, I was talking to my son's tutor about how I'd gotten back in touch with my old college chum Craig Bartlett and was planning to interview him as soon as the hoopla over Craig's new PBS children's cartoon *Dinosaur Train* had abated a bit. We chatted about Craig's early work in pioneering claymation at Will Vinton Studios in Portland, Oregon, and my son's tutor mentioned nostalgically that wonderful 1974 Will Vinton/Bob Gardiner classic of all claymation classics, *Closed Mondays*.

What he loved about it, he said, was the morphing you can do with claymation, the way one thing can magically turn into another without any break in credibility—because realism and surrealism are *equally believable* in clay.

Have you ever heard of Firesign Theater? They made surreal radio programs in the 1970s—not music or commentary, just stories exploring the possibilities of sound.

How Stories are Written

And I can't tell you how we loved them when I was a teen. We all had their records memorized, most particularly *Waiting for the Electrician or Someone Like Him* and *Don't Crush That Dwarf, Hand Me the Pliers*. My brother and I used to go to shallow seventies teen parties and sit in the corners being wallflowers and quoting Firesign Theater shtick to each other.

Like clay, sound can magically turn one thing into another as we listen. A horse whinnying behind the wavering voice of 'Tiny Dr. Tim' saying, "It's a horsey! Let's give the horsey a *sugar cube*," turns unexpectedly into a trumpeting elephant and thunders furiously away.

Great stuff, this playing with the eye of the mind!

And, just as with clay and sound, words can also magically turn one thing into another with no break in credibility.

We must use this to our full advantage. Zoom in on details—the protagonist is wearing argyle socks and playing obsessively with his wedding ring. Does our reader care if his hair's normal? That he's medium weight? That he has a 'nice' smile? *No.* They can guess all that for themself. They want a close-up of the chip in his front tooth, the tear in his screen door that lets in the mosquitoes he's always slapping, the mole on his neck that the secondary protagonist is going to spend a lot of time thinking about touching or not touching.

In fact, fantasy and sci-fi are popular genres precisely *because* we can mix fact and fiction so cleanly with words.

Whatever fiction genre we love, our medium—words— gives us the surreal ability to create absolutely anything we want to create.

This is our lodestone, writers. This is our magic wand.

Reviewing the Purpose of Storytelling

So we come to our story with a question: *"What's going to happen to these fascinating people in my head?"* And we spend hours, weeks, years exploring the answers—because there are myriad answers. There are almost *infinite* answers.

And the exploration of those answers—the long, glorious hours feeling our way through them as though blind, discovering which ones are right, when, where, in what way, and why—is our purpose in doing this work.

However, our reader comes to our story with a different question: *"Why should I care?"*

I learned this from the *Gormenghast* fantasy trilogy by Mervyn Peake, of which I read more than half in my early twenties at the behest of a friend. They're the quintessential blending of the real and surreal. Gormenghast is a castle as big as a city, which its inhabitants rarely leave. It's sprawling, ancient, *gothic*. Rats crawl in the dungeons, and bats fly around the belfries. Ivy covers the crumbling stone walls, and the furniture and draperies inside are tattered and dusty. The royal family is a collection of freaks—all except the youngest members, who are, against all odds, completely believable, emotional, multi-faceted.

Human.

Tell us a story about someone we've never met, but we'd love if we did. Someone interesting and funny and droll, but also baffled and clumsy and sometimes downright stupid. Someone whose life is weird and unexpected enough to be fascinating, while their reactions are ordinary enough to be poignantly familiar. Someone who screws up just like us, but handles it better than we do, who can fall over a footstool and land on their feet still walking, the eternal Dick Van Dyke.

How Stories are Written

Someone who hits bottom, bounces up, hits it again, bounces up again, hits it *again*, bounces so hard they knock a hole in the ceiling and wind up flying, arms and legs waving, into the ether.

Make their story unexpected but credible—startling but satisfying—something new and exciting everywhere they turn, but always completely coherent within the context of their own personal fictional dream.

And *keep them in the center* of that story, forever falling over footstools and landing on their feet.

I was enjoying *Gormenghast* enormously clear up until Fuschia Groan dies.

Fuschia isn't supposed to die! What was Peake thinking? She's the character I was reading for! Cranky and obstinate, but decent and feeling inside, she has all the qualities of a true sympathetic character. *Bang!* She hits bottom. *Bounce!* She goes flying. *Bang!* She hits bottom again. *Bounce!* She goes flying again. I loved the castle, sure. But I was reading for Fuschia.

Peake could go on designing traps for the other characters as long as he liked, but I quit reading *Gormenghast* the minute Fuschia disappeared.

Writer beware! Never forget: *we're storytellers*. We may think everyone knows that stories take a lot of words, that fiction is longer than oral storytelling by very virtue of the medium, and therefore our reader understands implicitly why they must hang on and keep reading and reading and reading this story we're so in love with. But the magic and flexibility of fiction are *always* submissive to the reader's investment.

Why should they care?

We must make our reader believe. But, even more than that, we must make them *want* to believe.

Chapter 4

Character Arc/Narrative Arc
The rainbow

Character arc: someone living their life
Narrative arc: the things that happen when someone lives their life

When I work with children, the first thing I do on the first day is review the basic parts of speech, grammatical points, stuff I know they probably already know. Then I teach them the very simple, straight-forward, zen fact: every sentence has a **subject** and a **verb**. Someone does something.

Subject. Verb. That's all there is to it. That's all they need to know.

I look at them. They look at me. I nod.

And then, *I mess with their heads.*

I tell them, "From this you can learn that all storytelling is holographic. Do you know what a holograph is? It's a document written entirely in the handwriting of the same person who signs it. A *whole* or *holistic* graph or piece of writing. And a holo*gram* is a picture made out of light, of which every little tiny bit is actually the whole big picture in miniature." I wave my hands around, showing them little-tiny and whole-big.

Character Arc/Narrative Arc

Then I say, "I think. Or the other way around. But, anyway, they're both very cool.

"Because a story—just like a sentence—has a subject and a verb: someone does something. And everything *in between* the big picture of the overall story and the tiny picture of the individual sentence has a subject and a verb. No matter what the granularity—cosmology to quantum mechanics—it's all designed the same. A subject and a verb."

Now, these children don't know what holographs, holograms, granularity, cosmology, or quantum mechanics are, but that's okay because I don't mind telling them. And kids love that! What cool ideas! It's not listening to a teacher drone on and on and on about participles and imperatives and the pluperfect, much less calling on them to parrot anything. They're bemused, but entertained. *When is she going to go back to drilling stuff into our heads?*

All those big words and concepts make subject-verb, frankly, laughably easy. Geez. Just two things stuck together. A person. And what they do. Anyone can remember *that*.

I like picturing the looks on their parents' faces when they go home after an hour with me and say, "Did you know a holo-something is something that's the same in its tiniest parts as it is in its biggest parts? And atoms are characters and what they do are verbs? And it has something to do with other stuff about writing too, but I forget what because I'm starting a novel?"

I love working with kids.

Character arc. Narrative arc. Subject. Verb. Someone does something.

So we're working on our story, living with these characters in our heads, hearing their voices speak to each other, watching them move around the rooms of their houses, the places they go, the wildernesses of city or forest or desert or small town ingrown like a toenail. And they're doing things (things they shouldn't), making decisions, taking trips, running into each other under inconvenient, embarrassing, or even dangerous circumstances. They're doing, doing, doing, and it keeps twisting back on them, thwarting them, turning their carefully or not-so-carefully laid plans inside out, tossing them cavalierly, time after time, out of the frying pan into the fire.

What are their *arcs*?

Well, *we* go through arcs. We go to a child's basketball game, maybe, and some kids there are mean to other kids, and we don't like it.

It sets up an internal conflict inside: we have our own personal issues about confrontation and control over other people and public situations and, maybe, our own experiences on the basketball court as children. And at the same time we have this dearly-cherished value that *we don't let people hurt kids*. Not if we have anything to say about it. So how do we resolve this internal conflict?

That's our character arc.

Meanwhile, this trigger to our character arc also sets off a domino effect, a series of events sparked by that original event. We go to the game, which causes us to see the kids being mean, which causes us to make a decision. Maybe we decide to hide our head and shuffle out in embarrassment. Maybe we decide to go along with the kids and pretend it's all fun and games. Maybe we decide to blow our top, and the police arrive. Maybe we decide on something else.

Whatever we decide causes another event, which backs us into a more specific corner, about which we must make a new, more refined decision, which narrows our options even more.

That's our narrative arc.

Character Arc/Narrative Arc

So the further we work our way through our character arc, the more focused our narrative arc becomes, and the more inevitable become the events we face. Until we reach the point after which the life we were leading before this chain of events (this narrative) came along has been irrevocably altered into something different (by our character).

Who's your story about? What's going on inside them that sets them up for this original decision with which they must cope throughout the rest of the story? What's on one side of their internal conflict—what *need* in their character forces them to make this particular decision? And what comes along and creates the conflicting side—what other need *contradicts* that original need, turning this one aspect of character into a narrative?

What values, beliefs, fears, hopes, prejudices, assumptions, secrets, denial, habits, and history bear in on this character constantly from all sides, forcing them to be able to react to stress in just the one way? What's the core of their internal conflict, the Gordian Knot, the inescapable toe-stubber beyond which they simply cannot continue? How does that core illuminate their two mutually-exclusive needs, the clues to their basic character and to how all of us—every single human on earth—live with irreconcilable paradox in our souls?

We must ask ourselves all of this every time we find ourselves dealing with internal conflict of our own. How we resolve the conflict matters less than what we learn about ourselves in dealing with it.

We're not just revealing characters when we create fiction. We're revealing the key to being human.

And what are the dominoes that keep falling on us or out from under our feet? What scenes occur, one after another, other characters coming in and out, days and nights passing, outside events happening, conversations, gestures, activities, *milestones in a life*?

We're not just chronicling stories when we write. We're chronicling the inevitable forward motion of being alive.

Chapter 5

Graphing in Three Dimensions
Theme

We can think of storytelling as (x,y,z) graphing, which is drawing an image through three-dimensional space with a single line, using two sets of coordinates: one for one end of the line, the other for the other. Computer graphics engineers write these (x_1,y_1,z_1) and (x_n,y_n,z_n), where n represents the furthest possible point at the end the line.

A character must make a journey through an experience in their life. That's a story. It can be either an outer or inner journey, with other characters or without them, but they must start at one point, and they must wind up at another point, and those two points encompass everything in between.

The protagonist's conflicting, overwhelming needs are the two diametrically-opposed points that define our x coordinates. Those needs get our protagonist through space in one dimension, which is their character arc.

The plot begins with a Hook and ends on a Climax, which are the two structurally-opposed points that define our y coordinates. That structure gets our protagonist through space on exactly the same journey in a *second* dimension, which is their narrative arc.

And our major and minor themes contain those aspects of life we're exploring through this story. We want more than one theme so we can create tension between them, and the two most powerful are defined by our z coordinates. They get our protagonist through space on that same journey in the *third* dimension, which is the progress of our exploration of themes.

You'll notice there are multiple points—an infinite number, actually—between the first and last sets of (x,y,z) coordinates, and at each of those points we must be able to define the coordinates of all three planes. For every step of our character arc, we must know the corresponding step in our narrative arc, which illuminate—all on their own—the corresponding step in the progress of our themes. That's (x,y,z).

Now, I'm not going to explicate theme, and this is on purpose. I have a Taoist perspective on theme. I believe the less said about it the better for everyone, especially the reader. We must focus on our storytelling—on developing truthful, gut-wrenching characters and believable, hair-raising plot—and forget about theme while we do it.

Then when we throw our reader off the rainbow into their own epiphany at the very end of our story...there they find the full illumination of our themes, the part we didn't know we knew, the art lying at the core of the craft of fiction.

When we have written our story and polished it in exactly the right way, we will have illuminated everything we have to say about these particular themes.

Let the reader be one to put them into other words.

Chapter 6

The Only Two Stories
Relationship & Quest

Mining Yourself

There are no new stories, only new perspectives.

Has anyone ever told you that? It's true.

There are two ways in this world to get into trouble: with other people and on our own.

If we want to get our protagonist into trouble with others, we give them a **relationship**. If we want to get them into trouble on their own, we give them a **quest**.

How many kinds of *relationship* are there? Well, there are romantic/sexual relationships (with women, with men), family relationships (with children, with parents, with siblings, with extended family), friendships (individual, group, crowd, close, distant, estranged), business relationships (with bosses, with subordinates, with peers, with allies, with competitors), and antagonists (original enemies or any of the above gone bad). We can also have relationships with things, as the narrator does in Marie Redonnet's *Hotel Splendid*, but unless they also involve either other people or a quest they're going to get boring pretty fast.

The Only Two Stories

How many kinds of *quest* are there? Two. The kind where we actually go somewhere, **external**, and the kind where we stay in one place, **internal**.

See? Only a handful.

So how do we write something new, something unique, something that wasn't already beaten to a fruity pulp long before we were even born?

These days everyone knows about Monty Python, that pillar of British non-sequitur and daftly logical conclusions. And many of us are even conversant with *The Meaning of Life*. But how many actually know the lyrics to *The Galaxy Song*?

Along with a plethora of cosmological facts (apparently first disproven and then re-proven, causing Eric Idle to demand 'the bastards' make up their minds), the song gives us that nihilistic reminder how amazingly unlikely were our births. And although it's meant, in context, to scare us, I for some reason have always found it rather encouraging.

After all, if my birth was amazingly unlikely—which isn't debated by scientists on either side of the argument—that means I'm unique, doesn't it? And if I'm unique, then my experience of life can't be duplicated by anybody, anywhere, at any point in history, can it? At least, not without my express written permission.

Take this to heart. *You are unique.*

We may have to paw through the minimalist slush pile of potential stories to find the ones that strike our fancy, but once we do we've got unlimited rein to do with them what we will.

Mine yourself.

No matter what story we want to tell, relationship or quest, we must look to our own lives to teach us how to tell it uniquely.

We must be alert wherever we go, whatever we do. There is only one person in history in a position to perceive and note down the specific, telling details of this life—nobody else's—in all their extraordinarily singular significance. Does cheese remind us of telephone wires because of our cheese-slicer? We give that to a character. When we're scared, do we finger our buttons? Some people do. When the one we love tells us they don't love us anymore, is our first thought of tango'ing off an Argentinian cliff to the anguished wail of Tito Luisardo?

Does it, in fact, inspire us to travel to Buenos Aires and there meet the ravishing grandson of Tito, who tells us of the secret *amor* of his grandfather and the violet-eyed Amelia Bence? Is it our passion for 1930s Argentinian music that teaches us, in its complex, magnificently-detailed, ultimately poignant way, what it means to be alive?

There is only one person who can discover the links between one detail and another that illuminate the workings of their own bizarrely convoluted human brain. (Have you ever seen a human brain? Convoluted doesn't even *begin* to cover it.) There is only one person who loves the unusual conglomeration of hobbies each of us loves in exactly the way we love them. There is only one person who will ever come up with the strange and unusual meanings each of us knows, in our heart of hearts, lie just beyond the surface of everything we do, everything we say, everything that ever happens around us.

It's not getting our books on a bookstore shelf that makes writing worthwhile. Believe me, I know.

It's getting to spend our writing time scrutinizing ourselves and our own lives for the devastating, electrifying, inherent beauty of living that is the essence of us—all that we will take with us to the grave.

The Only Two Stories

Differentiating Between Together & Alone

So the first thing we need to know is that writing itself is a quest, and if we don't know that when we first start out we sure will by the time it's done wrestling us to the floor.

A *quest* is a journey, external or internal, the solitary path that is the true path of each of us throughout our lives.

A *relationship*, on the other hand, is an accumulation of the consequences of people's influence upon each other, the mingling of individual paths that creates community between all of us out here rattling around in the world in the same place at the same time, social animals that we are. (This is, oddly, the act of publication—quite different and in some ways the opposite of writing.)

Is our story focused upon the characters and how they interact? Is it mainly about the ways in which these people relate to each other, how they come to signify to each other all things dreadful and ignoble and all things great and glorious, how they reach into each other's hearts and souls and rearrange the furniture to produce something new and unusual, something poignantly true to life, something none of them has ever been before?

That's a story of relationship.

Or is our story focused upon one character, one goal, one twisting, staggering, marvelous, and infuriating struggle to come to grips with what it means to be alone inside a single brainpan on this planet?

Yeah, that sounds like a quest to me.

Fyodor Dostoevsky's *The Brothers Karamozov* is a novel of relationships, the story of three brothers and a half-brother who struggle, in their different ways, to come to grips with each other and with the mysterious death of the father who has made their lives hell. It's a mystery, and as a mystery it involves the infinite permutations of human interactions, all the ways in which we move and breathe and behave around each other and create — in the act of creating our own lives — the world in which we all live.

On the other hand, Dostoevsky's *Crime and Punishment* is a quest. Again, there's a suspicious death, and again there's a search for some resolution to the crime. But in this case, there's no mystery. We know who committed the crime, how, and why, because we were there with him when he did it. Now we're learning all about what happens to a man who does such a thing — just an ordinary man, a mediocre man, someone with faults and virtues no better or worse than our own, but a man who has done something beyond the pale that now he can't undo. We are learning what the first step is for him, how this leads to the death and everything after, and by the end of the novel we learn how it turns out for him — what one man makes of this extraordinary act of character and how his goal (escaping punishment) twists around on him at the last moment and becomes something completely different from anything he could ever have predicted.

What about a story like the movie *Galaxy Quest*? Is it, in fact, a quest?

First, may I say to you: Enrico Colantoni? Tony Shalhoub? Sam Rockwell? Alan Rickman? Four of the great comic actors of our time, all in one place, all in one ludicrous, hilarious, death-defying spoof on *Star Trek*? Wow!

Ship's captain Jason Nesmith and his crew are the has-been stars of a science fiction TV show with all the overweening schmaltz and cliché of the original *Star Trek*. They're living off their fading fame making appearances in malls and shopping center parking lots across America. It's a hard time to have no talent except a surprising ability to conquer the galaxy.

There's a Hook (Jason makes a fool of himself at a sci-fi convention, in a spoof on a *Saturday Night Live* shtick starring William Shatner). There are Developments (aliens co-opt the whole kit-&-caboodle to save their planet from Sarris, the Darth Vader of Reptilia). And there's a Climax (Sarris wins! Oh, *no*!). There's also a Resolution, which is of course the feel-good moment at the end of the story.

Throughout the plotline, the characters mess with each other's heads, save each other's butts, and come a cropper of each other's failings. In the end, they have all learned something significant about themselves and each other and had a *darn* good time, to boot.

They have changed each other.

This is a story of relationship.

Graham Greene's *The End of the Affair,* on the other hand, while it purports to be about a man and a woman involved in an illicit romance during the bombing of London in World War II, isn't actually about the affair at all. The reader follows Maurice through the years after Sarah inexplicably dumps him, digging deeper and deeper into his own character, until he learns not only the long-buried truth about the end of their affair but the truth about himself—the one person he hasn't thought to confront all along.

This is a solitary journey into the very heart of what it means to live alone in a human soul.

This is a quest.

Molding & Being Molded By Relationship

There's a legend that after Faulkner left Hollywood someone found a piece of paper in the garbage can by his desk that said repeatedly all the way down the page: "Boy meets girl. Boy meets girl. Boy meets girl."

This is a take-off on the standard romance plot, "Boy meets girl. Boy loses girl. Boy gets girl."

And, sexism aside, that's the basic issue behind all relationship stories: meet someone, lose them, regain them.

The purpose of relationship stories is the exploration of the ways in which human beings, thrown together as we are on this increasingly-crowded planet, alter and reinforce and form each other's lives even as we are formed. We might each start out alone in our own little squished post-natal heads, and we might, indeed, spend our time in this mortal coil isolated inside those heads, which is the whole point of the quest story and the point of writing in general.

But the time we spend here *itself* forces us into proximity with others so, unless we check out the minute we check in, our fate is the fate of all co-existing substances: to mold and be molded in turn. (Which, as it happens, is exemplified in the practice of publication.)

If a story is a full action with a point, then the point of a relationship story is whatever the writer finds significant in that relationship.

The entire history of a relationship, like the history of a life, is generally random and really quite boring unless it's designed specifically around significance.

Therefore the full action is: the beginning of the significant part of the relationship, through the significant developments, to that one thing the writer wants to say is significant about this particular relationship.

In **mystery, horror,** and **thriller**, what is significant is who did or does what to whom and *why*. As mystery writers are so fond of saying, "Show me the why, and I'll show you the who." While some mysteries, horror stories, and thrillers explore the potential for danger in us all, many are less discerning—they can be about any type of threat, on any kind of flimsy grounds (and some are really flimsy), so long as they explore why people do things to each other.

Edgar Allan Poe and Wilkie Collins gave us the original Western mysteries (although the Chinese have been telling mystery stories for 2,000 years), while Horace Walpole gave us the original gothic romance, which is the basis of horror, which is the basis of thriller. And those darn resilient genres haven't met their untimely ends yet.

In a **romance** what is significant is the sexual energy between people. As we all know, sex is the single greatest motivator in the Animal Kingdom. It would have to be, wouldn't it? Any species that *wasn't* designed specifically around sex would simply find procreation far too difficult and die out in a generation. (Have you ever given birth to the next generation? It's *hard*!) This is why romance has been and remains one of the all-time massive-selling genres in fiction. Nobody ever gets tired of thinking about sex, especially its powerful emotional ramifications, which in romance we are pleased to call love.

Emily and Charlotte Bronte, Jane Austen, and—much later—Jean Rhys laid the groundwork for all modern romance stories.

In a **buddy** story what is significant is the ability of two or more people to bond to each other above and beyond the confines of family—overcoming the plethora of differences between us, but without the magnetism of sex—to find a deeper meaning in that human bond. We need each other. Even when we sometimes can't stand each other, we still need each other.

Interestingly, most of the earliest novels that might have been buddy stories are, in fact, quests: *Don Quixote*, *Moll Flanders*, *Tom Jones*. Fascinated as we are by bonding, buddy stories lack either death or sex and therefore typically need more plot than just the relationship to carry them all the way through to a Climax. So instead we use layering—multiple purposes—to explore the eternal greater truths.

The mystery duo Sherlock and Watson are buddies. The Japanese 'Western' *The Seven Samurai* is a buddy story. Mary Shelley's classic sci-fi novel *Frankenstein*, weirdly, is the story of what happens when we try to build our own buddy.

In a **family** drama the significance lies in the many ways in which family members create, influence, and infect the life they all must share. Family is our original tribe. We are a social species, and our brains are organized to find gossip, intrigue, and conflicting agendas interesting as all get-out.

Eudora Welty went to the wall with *Delta Wedding*, but before her we had Emily Bronte, Ivy Compton-Burnett, Faulkner, and James Thurber's hilarious *My Life and Hard Times*. Rebecca West wrote the extraordinary *Cousin Rosamund* trilogy as a fictionalized account of her own family.

And in a **parent-child** story what is significant is the special power imbalance between parents and children and how that sets the participants up for conflict and union more fundamental to character than any other relationship.

Thus we get fairytales and their enormous dependence upon parent-child relationships: mothers, fathers, step-parents, runaway children, lost children, obedient children, disobedient children, dominated and dominating children. In many cultures, the royal family serves as the archetype of the nuclear family for fairytales, laying the groundwork for fiction and storytelling in general.

It's especially effective if we can combine several of these stories into one. Almost any story—even William Gibson's geek sci-fi classic *Neuromancer*—gets more exciting if we add romance.

So what about the plot structure of the relationship story: meet someone, lose someone, gain someone?

In modern culture—after the rise of the romantic eighteenth-century concept that we might choose whom we spend time with rather than simply take what we get—we find ourselves especially drawn to that act of choosing. This means the beginning of the relationship.

But all stories need conflict. It's not enough to say: "They met and lived happily ever after." I mean, what kind of story is *that*? Remember, the reader wants to read about when things go wrong.

So it must be: "They met, they were prevented from being together, they triumphed over their obstacles, and *then* they lived happily ever after." Frankly, once we get to the triumph, nobody's even interested in the happily-ever-after. That's why we can cram it all into one phrase like that. "Whatever."

This, of course, lends itself very tidily to the standard plot structure for all stories: Hook (they meet or are reunited after a separation), Development through a sequence of Conflicts of rising tension to a Faux Resolution (separation, reunion, separation, reunion, *big* separation, *big* reunion!), and Climax (insurmountable obstacle to their union—oh, dreadful day, they can never be together *again*). And the Resolution: either they never will be together again, or somehow they magically manage to surmount the insurmountable to triumph over the ultimate separation.

And that, my friend, is the whole point of this story. I could have told you how it ended in the first place, but it wouldn't have been nearly as much fun, now, would it?

Aiming Past Ecstasy through Quest

I had a great conversation with a client one day on the subject of *Galaxy Quest,* which, it turned out, is one of both our favorite movies.

My client made the good point that a quest has an *aim*. In the story of a relationship, what seems to be the aim is really only the locus of a framework, within which the author explores humanity and its infinite disgrace and glory. While, in the story of a quest, the aim really *is* the point.

In a quest, the protagonist is driven relentlessly forward toward their aim, through punishment and reward, trauma and reprieve, until they reach it and *in reaching that aim* discover what lies beyond it.

Although an entire lifetime could, theoretically, be framed as a quest (remember *Don Quixote, Moll Flanders, Tom Jones*), the bildungsroman is rarely today considered a viable storytelling format, which means the quest itself becomes the tidy storytelling framework, good for all themes and seasons.

The complete action is: the beginning of the quest, through the significant developments, all the way to the aim or at least destruction of the quest.

An **external quest** is the easiest to design—we send our protagonist on an **adventure.** Such stories are riveting for the details of new and unusual places. It's the Marco Polo experience of learning, the tidal wave of new information about what kind of planet this is, who lives here besides us, what they're like. When we write such a quest, the bulk of the work is the research. We must go where our protagonist goes, learn what they learn. And, like Marco Polo, we bring our findings back with us to share with our reader.

Our protagonist must have a reason for this adventure — storytelling is always about cause-&-effect. They must have an aim to accomplish, a reason for ending their adventure (unless we do something fancy like ending on the realization that this particular adventure will never end). And things must happen to them on this adventure.

It's not enough to take a guess at what the adventure is like. Unless we're writing fantasy, our readers can guess just as well as we can, and they do not come to writers for anything they can do themselves. Mrs. Radcliffe, the nineteenth-century English blockbuster author of such grand gothic epics as *The Mysteries of Udolpho*, is reported to have lifted entire pages of description out of travel books for the foreign settings of her characters' travails. Now, that is of course very bad manners. (Mrs. Radcliffe.) And today we would get busted. But she did demonstrate her solid understanding of the need for authentic telling detail.

The purpose of an external quest, an adventure, is to go somewhere. The external quest has a geographical aim. And whether or not the protagonist actually gets there, coming to grips with that destination is the point of telling this particular story.

An **internal quest**, on the other hand, is often more powerful but much more subtle. Our protagonist's character arc itself is the adventure — who are they in the beginning, what happens to alter them in the crucible of life, wherein lie their hopes, wherein their climactic despair?

An internal quest is concerned, on all levels, with the resolution of the protagonist's unresolved needs. *They need something.* Naturally, all protagonists do, but an internal quest must be designed to keep those needs clear and alive in the protagonist's perspective. In other types of stories, those needs can be subsumed into actions, complications, the interplay between one character's needs and another's. In an internal quest those needs are the be-all and end-all of the story. And the protagonist's drive to meet those needs is the aim.

In the relationship story *Pride and Prejudice*, Jane Austen can, in the interests of true love, cavalierly toss aside Elizabeth's powerful need to make snap judgments, which has motivated her throughout the novel. But in Henry James' quest story, "The Aspern Papers," the nameless protagonist must either acquire the papers or resolve his emotional need for them in a way that allows him to live out his life without being emotionally destroyed.

Like a relationship story, any quest fits very nicely into standard plot structure: Hook (aiming at something), Development through a sequence of Conflicts of rising tension to a Faux Resolution (danger of failure, averted, danger again, averted, *big* danger, *big* success! maybe the protagonist will just pitch a permanent tent?), and Climax (*impossible danger of failure*, this quest must end in complete and utter disaster!). And the Resolution: either the quest ends entirely unexpectedly, or somehow the impossible danger is averted and the quester safely achieves their aim.

In this way, the protagonist of a quest discovers, in the end, not the interdependence of humanity in all its infinite entanglements and permutations. Not even the dichotomy—the release or ecstasy—they expected.

But only, in the final hour, a deeper understanding of their own life, after all.

Chapter 7

Reading with Attention
Learning your form

Reading for Plot Design

I love vintage mysteries—those cheap, battered little paperbacks of the 1930s, forties, and fifties—and I've just spent the past year scouring the West Coast for them in all the obscure bookshops I could find between San Francisco and Portland. So now I've got hundreds of pulp mysteries to work my way through. It's a *pulp avalanche*.

And as I fly through these—I'm reading almost one a night—I've devised a reading exercise for the study of their structure, which I've assigned to my local teenage creative writing students and I'm going to assign to you, too.

Whatever book you're reading right this very minute, take a quick second to look in the back and see how many pages it has. Rounded, I mean. A lot of these early mysteries are in the 180-240 range, but nowadays novels are expected to be actually quite long by comparison, in the 280-400 range. This has to do with the shift from general-purpose novels to strictly genre fiction in recent decades, mega-volume fantasy and series fiction pushing the envelope right to the limit and beyond into

Reading with Attention

the infinite abyss, as well as a growing neglect of the editorial craft of cutting and trimming by many publishers. (No wonder we suddenly need flash fiction.)

We'll find a scrap of paper or a used envelope and jot this down at the bottom: total number of pages.

Now we'll divide that into: $1/8, 1/6, 1/4, 1/3, 1/2, 2/3, 3/4, 5/6, 7/8$. We can knock it right down into all the eighths and sixths if we like, but these are the main divisions. Scribble those numbers vertically above the total.

Now—as we work our way through our current read, every time we come to one of those pages, we'll make a note of whatever big, important plot point is going on *right there*. At least within a few pages.

Depending upon the type of novel we're reading (and in some cases how recently it was written), the Climax may be shoved all the way to within spitting distance of the last page. And that's fine! That's an excellent way to end a novel. So when we get to the Climax, we go ahead and scribble that down, too. We can give it its page number if we like or, if the Resolution really is negligible, just let it roll with the final page number.

We label it at the top with the title of the book. Then throw it on a box on our desk and start a new scrap for the next book.

Eventually, we're going to have a whole *raft* of these little lists.

And. They. Are. Priceless.

We take them out every now and then to study. What do we see?

Act 1

Hook (the beginning to $1/8$-$1/6$)
Conflict #1 ($1/8$-$1/6$ to $1/4$-$1/3$)

Act 2
Conflict #2 ($1/4$-$1/3$ to $1/2$-$2/3$)
Conflict #3 ($1/2$-$2/3$ to $2/3$-$3/4$)

Act 3
Faux Resolution ($2/3$-$3/4$ to $5/6$-$7/8$)
Climax ($5/6$-$7/8$ to the climax near the end)

Writers will joggle this a bit. Sometimes there are mini- and midi-Faux-Resolutions at the ends of Conflict #1 and Conflict #2, a little pacing to give each element punch, although they're often truncated in mid-stride by the hook to the next Conflict. And sometimes the Hook is a bit shorter and Conflict #1 closer to the beginning to make room for a longer Conflict #2, or vice versa. (That's only by some small number of pages, though, not huge chunks.)

Some writers use a pattern based on quarters ($1/8$, $1/4$, $1/2$, $3/4$, $7/8$), while others prefer a pattern based on thirds ($1/6$, $1/3$, $1/2$, $2/3$, $5/6$). Occasionally I stumble across someone who skews the $1/2$ point to $3/5$ (rare) or even $2/3$ (even more rare).

Some writers also trim the Faux Resolution down to a single page before they kick their characters off the moving train into the hook for the Climax, while others drag the Faux Resolution out a bit to shove the Climax farther toward the last page.

That's why this isn't formula, it's structure. A house with many rooms is just as livable as a house with only one room, but a house with no supporting walls at all falls down. Once we've tracked the structure through several entire novels, we develop a nose for it. Just keep an eye on those fractions.

So let's lick a pencil and scrabble for whatever's handy. All those novels we've been reading all these years?

All structured properly.
You're going to be *amazed*.

Reading for Character Development

Now I'm also going to assign a *second* exercise for our current reading material. Because I don't believe in doing things halfway.

We'll flip over that scrap of paper or used envelope on which we're jotting down our plot design research and scribble the name of the protagonist of whatever we're reading on the back. If there's more than one protagonist, we'll scribble the name of the main one. We'll chew our pencil for a few minutes (don't eat the paint—just destroy the little metal bit that holds the eraser) and ask ourselves, "What does this character *need* more than anything else in the entire world?" When we've got it, we'll write it down under their name. "And what do they need that *conflicts* with this need?" We'll write that down too. Put a big blocky square all the whole thing.

Got it?

Good.

Now, every time we reach one of those milestones we outlined on the other side of this paper, we'll jot down on this side *what happens to the protagonist and their conflicting needs*. I can guarantee something does.

Is one need satisfied in some partial but slightly fulfilling way? Just enough to keep them addicted to the search for total fulfillment?

Is their search for fulfillment of one need thwarted in some way? Enough to freak them out, but not enough to make them think, "This is for the birds. I'm giving up"?

Are their needs ever totally fulfilled?

Are their needs ever totally thwarted?

Scribble, scribble, scribble. We do our scribbling. We're scribblers.

Then—you knew I was going to say this—we chuck it in that box on our desk. And start the whole thing over again with another book.

When we're ready, we'll take these scraps out of the box and study them. What patterns do we see? How do all these different authors lead their characters by the nose through the hoops that have been set for them, feeding their needs, denying their needs, feeding their needs again, denying their needs again? How does this rhythm build to a crescendo by the end, driving both character and reader nuts with frustration and anticipation?

How have these authors kept their reader *addicted*?

Do you ever watch fireworks—for Chinese New Year, Mexican Independence, a hobbit's eleventy-first birthday?

Every time I do, I'm thinking how it would feel to have them go off inside my heart. Then I think about how all these authors make the Climaxes of their novels feel...

Exactly. That. Way.

Chapter 8

Creating Reader Addiction
Tension

Creating the Basic Tension in Character

Let's talk reader addiction. Let's find out why some stories can hold sway over the imaginations of hundreds of thousands of readers for generations, while others vanish without a whimper almost before they're read.

Let's take a look at character tension, the inherent tension inside a single character that must, eventually, cause them to collide with themself.

Internal conflict.

I'm working with a client right now on a Middle Grade (MG) novel in which a main character must become romantically entangled with one of the villains. At the same time, one of the major events involves that character turning their back on that villain, in a last-minute switcheroo that allows them to win a major triumph for the protagonist's side.

But then the character has to turn *back* to that villain, in order to set up the Faux Resolution that leads to the Climax. It's a whole sequence of unbreakable cause-&-effect to make a Superhero weep. And it has to be *perfect*.

Creating Reader Addiction

How do we do it?

With internal conflict.

The part about being romantically-attracted to the villain is easy for the later MG audience. Those people are pre-pubescent, just beginning to sprout hormones, and it's a big surprise to them to discover themselves feeling irresistible urges to consort romantically with the opposite sex.

So all we need to do for this story is show how this character is swept off their feet by the villain in a romantic tsunami that takes them completely by surprise and writes their doom in indelible ink all over their face. We've all been there.

But at the same time, we need to show how this character *manages to break with* this overwhelming romantic attachment at the crucial moment. And what drives that break?

It has to be that character's fundamental *need*, the need that shapes their personality, fuels their journey forward through the plot, makes them who they are. What kinds of things serve as character need?

What kinds of things serve as *ours*?

Well, we all need love and acceptance. And we tend to choose one of a handful of basic avenues toward satisfying that need:

affection
intelligence
work
talent
self-protection
self-promotion
self-deprecation
power
money

humor

tragedy

mystery

There are others, but these are some of the biggest. We all strive toward certain stations along the track of that universal Love & Acceptance Train.

Say we've got a character who needs *affection*. Affection is what gains them love and acceptance. So this character's basic, driving agenda is to *get affection from people*. Anything that interferes with that agenda gets tossed by the wayside. Obstacles are never taken seriously, detours are always hijacked, arguments are just so much babbling in the wind.

"Don't try to get affection out of *her*," the other characters cry, aghast. "She's got a knife in her pocket!"

"Don't stand in my way," this character yells belligerently. "She's got the manna I need!"

While, at the same time, someone *else* is maybe sporting the ever-popular hormone flag.

Whom to choose? This quandary gives our character devastating internal conflict.

Or say we've got a character who needs to be *self-deprecating*. Advertising their own failings is just their thing — it's what makes their life, oddly enough, worth living. This is a tricky protagonist to pose, because self-deprecators tend to be victims, and victims are boring. Nobody wants to read about a boring protagonist.

But let's say this character isn't a victim, they're actually quite forceful and entertaining and full of beans. But there it is: they need to be, above all things, self-deprecating.

This can get them into a *whole lot of trouble*.

"You're tall and handsome!" gushes Eve Arden.

Creating Reader Addiction

"You're near-sighted," Groucho shoots back (*A Day at the Circus*).

Groucho can get away with this because the vast suspension of disbelief in 1930s comedy audiences left him plenty of room to continue romancing the woman in all good faith in spite of his self-castigating one-liners. But a modern fictional character must remain faithful to their agenda, so when they need to self-deprecate, god help them, they need to *self-deprecate*. And when the survival of all they hold dear depends entirely upon them accepting the role of hero, they're going to get themself into some mighty hot water shucking the cape over and over again.

Princess Leia says she'd prefer to kiss a wookie, which Han Solo says he's willing to arrange. At the same time they both desperately need other things—she needs the rebellion to succeed, and he needs to watch out for Number One. And so their romance struggles and struggles and struggles to get off the ground, until he's being dropped into carbon-freeze and she has only seconds to admit *she'll do anything* to get him safely out again. (Just in case hers is the first face he sees when he's unfrozen, so he won't throw her through a wall.)

It's too bad they didn't say in the first place, "I love you, and you love me. Let's go kick some interstellar ass."

But no.

Or say we've got a character who needs to be *mysterious*. It's simply how they style themself. It's their personal fetish. So when it comes time to trust, they don't trust the ones who could make their lives so much easier. And when it comes time to divulge secrets, they never divulge them in time. And when it comes time to put their life in the hands of someone who has *also* made it their mission to hide the truth about themself...they can't bring themself to do it.

Which means this need to be mysterious is going to constantly trip them up in their pursuit of whatever *other need* we've laid at their door.

Jane Austen's *Emma* is so busy rushing around playing matchmaker she never has to admit her own secret romantic needs—until her machinations lead her to wreck her own chances.

Internal conflict comes from dual, opposing needs. No matter what happens in a story, our protagonist's fundamental conflicting *needs* keep them from achieving the aim they've set themselves to achieve and, even worse, force them into the nightmare they so desperately want to avoid.

This is what makes our characters addictive to the reader.

And addiction is what keeps them turning the pages long past midnight, gripping our books in their hot, sweaty palms, hoovering up our words like little human vacuum cleaners.

Creating the Basic Tension in Plot

One of the things I love about fiction is that craft is craft, and what works for one particular genre actually works, in a very fundamental way, for all genres. It's funny how the arts can be so convenient.

So let's examine plot tension now, the inherent tension between two disparate plotlines that must eventually cause them to collide.

External conflict.

Every story is the story of more than one intertwining plotline. Genre fiction is kind of fun because we can twine plotlines from different genres, and when we're done we've mixed genres, like *The Color Kittens*, and come up with something new.

Creating Reader Addiction

Every story is the story of how two plotlines run *almost* parallel from beginning to end, only to collide in a stunning display of fireworks at the Climax.

Think of those plotlines as railroad tracks.

In **mystery**, those two plotlines are the unraveling of what *really* happened in the context of what *appears* to have happened. The Climax is the point at which the detective or seeker-for-truth seems to be almost tricked into believing that what *appears* to have happened is in fact what *really happened*, and they are suddenly proven to be, in the immortal words of Poirot, 'such an eediot!' So when they pull a rabbit out of their hat the reader unexpectedly understands the entire story from the opposite side of the tapestry.

In **horror** and **thriller**, it's the same thing except both plotlines are occurring simultaneously and there's enormous pressure upon the protagonist to sort them out before something dire occurs.

In **fantasy**, those two plotlines are generally the paths of good and evil (or, in the versions I prefer, between fantasy and reality or between two conflicting fantasies). The Climax is the point at which evil triumphs (or chaos triumphs, or deconstruction triumphs), throwing the protagonist into an impossible state of existence from which, when they extricate themself, they find they're living in unforeseen harmony between either fantasy and reality or those two conflicting fantasies. They hope!

In **science-fiction** those two plotlines are generally two paths *toward* the perceived future and *away* from that future. The Climax is the point at which those two struggles reach their inevitable point of stasis, where the tension between them exceeds capacity and the break throws the protagonist into the *worst possible* future so that, when they re-orient themself, they discover an extraordinary new way of coping with the future as it really is.

In **romance**, those two plotlines are generally the protagonist's and the nemesis/lover's conflicting searches for whatever it is they're after. (It could be anything, but when we mix genres to come up with a significant conflicting need we make this one especially powerful.) The Climax is the point at which those searches bring the two inevitably together in conflict, where the clash of agendas throws them both top-over-teakettle so that, when they come back upright, they discover they're in love.

In **commercial fiction,** it's all the same except everything that happens could, conceivably, happen to the average reader.

And in **literary fiction,** this is all done exactly the same way only with meticulous attention to language.

The issue to keep in mind is that those two plotlines, because they are different plotlines (and we make them as different as we possibly can, so the fireworks will be really impressive), contain an inherent tension between them. "You are not I," said Paul Bowles. Which is the basic tension of all human existence.

So when we set our protagonist on these paths of self-destruction, the reason they're paths of self-destruction is that the character must simultaneously cope with two conflicting agendas. And they're going to discover—in the long run and exactly when they can *least* afford it—that those two conflicting agendas are irreconcilable.

Up until then, sure, there've been glancing collisions, there's been damage, there've been sparks...but there was always hope of reconciling those two agendas.

The Climax is here to prove: there will be no reconciliation.

Creating Reader Addiction

Write toward that Climax. Set your characters off down their road to hell, paved so lovingly with attractions no reader in their right mind could resist. Let your characters round corners and scare the wits out of themselves when they catch glimpses of where they're really going. Then let them round more corners—complications—after which they lose sight of the game.

Keep them moving, always moving toward the collision they have no idea is coming.

And in the last conflict before that collision occurs, (Conflict #3) give them one extra push.

Increase the incline.

Now, *that's* tension.

Chapter 9

Creating Reader Fulfillment
Resonance

Touching Your Reader's Core with Resonance

A client brought up a good point in the comments one day when we were talking about not introducing a pivotal character too late in the story. She wanted to know: "When is too late too late?"

The truth is the sooner we introduce our essential characters, the better the **resonance** when our Climax (featuring those characters) wraps back around to where they first appeared. Make your wrap *big*. Make your wrap *loooooong*. A wrap of twenty pages—or even 100 pages—isn't worth it to the reader when there are writers out there managing wraps of 200, 300, 400 pages or more. Readers *love* resonance.

But what does that mean?

You know those period-piece movies about the 1920s where everyone goes to some fabulously rich, fabulously isolated house together, and they're all scurrying around in the middle of the night in clinging ankle-length sequins and cummerbunds, their wrists at shoulder-height, uttering noises that should by rights be coming out of rodents?

Creating Reader Fulfillment

Those houses that are all dark, carved staircases and crackling fireplaces and Persian rugs, where someone is bound to come tumbling down the stairs at some point and land dead at the feet of the heroine in the front hall?

I *love* those darn movies.

And one thing you'll notice (this has nothing to do with the movie plots, by the way) is that those houses are usually decorated in a pastiche of Oriental imports in brass and cloisonné.

The absolutely best part is the enormous brass gong in the front hall.

They used those gongs to sound the alarm to get dressed-up in your fanciest knickers for formal dinner every night, then twenty minutes later to call the cattle down to the trough. However, if I'd been around I'd have stood there bonging that thing all evening simply for the joy of the **resonance.**

Resonance is how we reach out of the pages, through the words, past the reader's intellectual appreciation of our story, and touch their very core. It is the essence of storytelling — creating a visceral response in the reader.

In technical terms, resonance is when something happens late in the story that reminds the reader of something that happened earlier in the story and creates a link between those two events to illuminate the hidden essence of both.

Remember in *The Art & Craft of Fiction: A Practitioner's Manual* when we talked about looking for the **links** between two disparate things to reveal a fundamental truth about life inherent to both? How that's the basis of all art?

This is the technique for doing that through structure. (There are dozens of aspects to linking truths — structure is only one.)

When two things resonate, they automatically include everything between them, just like a gong. So if we have a significant object that turns up in Chapter 7 and we repeat it in Chapter 9, the reader forms an unconscious mental link between its appearance in Chapter 7 and its other appearance in Chapter 9, and the pages between take on an incredibly subtle ambience of a united episode. If we have an event that happens in Chapter 3 and something related happens in Chapter 10 and again in Chapter 19 and again in Chapter 31, the reader begins to build (unconscious) associations in their mind between these chapters, making them milemarkers for where our story is going. (If we've got 50 chapters, and this series of milemarkers ends in Chapter 31, we've either made our point or dropped the ball.)

And if we have a character who turns up in Chapter 1 and then reappears under extraordinarily significant circumstances in the Climax—that character has enormous *resonance*.

Can we get away with a character vital to the Climax who *doesn't* have resonance?

In *Jane Eyre*, her secret cousin Stuffed-Shirt St. John is wildly significant to the Climax, in which Jane must choose between either marrying him and becoming a missionary in the wilds of—I don't know, some ancient culture the Brits of the nineteenth century thought was primitive because they hadn't invented scones—or going back to that decrepit, blinded old rascal Rochester and taking care of *him* instead.

But was this a real predicament? Did Charlotte Bronte have the reader on the edge of their seat over Jane's decision?

Heck, no. St. John only appears in the last portion of the novel, while Rochester has been lurking in the bushes since barely a fifth of the way in—a sixth, even, if we count him as a rumor.

Creating Reader Fulfillment

When Jane goes back to Rochester, everything between their first and final meetings begins to vibrate with an inner life of its own, created by the verification of what the reader suspected in the first place—Rochester is essential. However, when Jane gives St. John the old heave-ho (and St. John's fate—even his words—gets the premiere spot actually closing the novel), nobody even notices.

But what about mysteries and thrillers? Doesn't the culprit remain invisible until the grand unveiling in the Climax?

In my first mystery they sure did. No matter how many times I read that story through—and it's a pretty good story, with high tension, strong cause-&-effect, three-dimensional characters—it just didn't *work*. Until I found a way to slip the culprit in on page two. Suddenly! Resonance.

So how late is too late?

In the mystery canon it's spelled out for us: all essential characters must appear in Act I, within the first quarter-to-third of the story. And we would all do well to abide by that guideline.

We must know who our main characters are (this seems obvious, but a lot of the time 'pantsers'—those optimistic little critters writing by the seat of their pants—actually have no idea), and know who is essential to our Climax. Then we think of some way to show their faces somewhere in the early chapters (the first quarter to third of our story). They don't have to stick around. The protagonist doesn't even have to meet them. But we must get them in there, and let the reader imprint on them, even in the most delicate, fleeting way.

Alec D'Urberville, the ruin of Tess, makes only a handful of appearances in her life. But he is there at the Climax, just as he is there in Chapter 5 to show his face for the first time, when he starts the dreadful chain of obsession that eventually, in the end, catches her in its monstrous knot.

Playing Fair with Resonance

I'm reading an Ellery Queen today, after a whole pile of other pulp mysteries, and I've also started re-reading *Hillary Waugh's Guide to Mystery & Mystery Writing*. Waugh was one of the great American mystery authors of the twentieth century (he died only a couple of years ago), and he dissected the mystery genre with great insight and intelligence.

One of the things he discusses is a crucial aspect that was missing from some (but not all) of Edgar Allan Poe's seminal works, from which the entire Western mystery genre sprang, "The Murders in the Rue Morgue," "The Mystery of Marie Roget," "The Purloined Letter," "Gold Bug," and "Thou Art The Man":

Fair Play.

But what is Fair Play?

Fair Play is letting the reader know what's going on. Even more than that, Fair Play is planting the clue to the solution early—preferably on one of the first pages.

Now, the general understanding of Fair Play is that we have to do it to keep the reader's loyalty. If we don't Play Fair, the reader gets mad at us and goes away. Birdcages throughout the ages have been papered with books by writers who ignored the Rule of Fair Play.

But Fair Play has an even more important job than that. After all, writers get away with *all kinds of crap* with their readers, and if they're good enough writers the readers take it, pay for it, and keep coming back for more. No. Fair Play is based on something even closer to the reader's heart than fairness, and that is...

Having a good time.

As an Australian friend of mine discovered when he visited me years ago in downtown San Francisco, a grand adventure, whether real or fictional, is all about having a good time.

Whatever else goes on in our story, our reader wants to *enjoy the experience of reading it.*

Of course, people's ideas of enjoyment vary widely, and readers in general tend to enjoy a lot more of being ejected from their chairs, dragged around, thrown against the walls, and smacked silly than you'd ever believe.

But, more than anything else, readers enjoy resonance.

That's when they get to the end of the story and find there, unexpectedly and yet inevitably, the beginning of it. That clue the writer planted on the early pages.

Putting our reader inside that brass gong and giving it a good, hearty *clang*.

Readers love this! It's possibly the single most important reason for the popularity of mysteries throughout the past 150 years. A devastating event. And the key to that event.

Give the reader a whiff of something tantalizing, lead them a merry chase in all the wrong directions, and then smack them in the face with the whole tantalizing pie.

It's that wonderful, visceral sense of familiarity, that whisper in the back of the mind: *this ending was inevitable.* It's the seductive implication that, if they'd just paid close enough attention (and they will the next time they read it, they promise themself!) they could have figured the ending out before we showed it to them. It's that magical authorial sleight-of-hand, creating a positive emotional response in the reader by what we've left out as much as what we've put in.

Planting a clue to the Climax in a story's Hook is the simplest, most powerful fiction technique I know.

It makes the story a relentless progression always forward toward a Climax both unexpected and inevitable, a living, breathing thing in the reader's hands, the story of an ending that appears to have been manifested out of thin air by sheer genius.

Chapter 10

Drawing an Analogy
Step by step

Drawing a Logo

I'm going to draw an analogy for you now. So please bear with me.

One Saturday last year my husband and I spent the whole day creating a logo for the publishing press we invented to publish my first book on writing, *The Art and Craft of Fiction: A Practitioner's Manual*.

I wanted to use an icon of my childhood for the logo, a cardboard cut-out advertisement for a festival dated 1899. It's the head of a young blond woman in an enormous hat with violet ostrich feathers, her arms clad in soft leather gloves from elbow to fingertip, her hands to her face, resting her chin thoughtfully on one finger. She's gazing up as though admiring the ceiling. Her name — in overly-elegant nineteenth century script under her elbows — is La Favorita.

My family found her hanging on the wall of an hacienda in the Ecuadorian countryside where we lived for two years while I was growing up. My parents moved her to a prominent spot in the hacienda dining room and photographed her for

Drawing an Analogy

posterity, and by the time we left she had become a *de facto* member of the family. La Favorita hangs in a frame right now in my mother's living room, her cardboard face 110 years old and still fresh as a girl.

When I told my mother what we wanted to do for the logo of my press, she sent me the original photograph of La Favorita, and we scanned it. Unfortunately, it turned out she's got far too much detail and shading to work as a tiny little spine logo. We tried shrinking her down, and my son loved it, but from a distance of two feet she just looked like a grey blob.

So we set to work turning her into a piece of art that would work.

My husband and I sat side-by-side on the couch all day while he Photoshopped La Favorita into a line drawing. She needed enough big dark elements to be recognizable at a casual glance—even tiny—but she also needed her itsy-bitsy little facial features to show up with their soulful gaze. We blacked in her hat and gloves (although the gloves have wonderful highlighted wrinkles in the soft leather) and exaggerated her eyes and mouth. We erased all of her from chin to gloves and then went back, meticulously re-creating only those lines absolutely necessary to give her definition. She has a lot of ruffles around her face, which looked weird when they disappeared. We had to get just enough of them in to remove the weird without competing with her more important elements.

The *pièce de résistance* turned out to be not even a part of her, but the shadow her cardboard cut-out cast on the wall when she was photographed. It's only behind one arm (the light came from an angle), but it's a lovely calligraphic line that thins and thickens as it goes around the curves of her sleeve.

We sharpened it up. Then we looked at her other arm, which has no such line. We paused.

We were going to flip the line and use its opposite on the other side.

But then I remembered a fascinating fact about stylized images: what the eye knows should be there it will see *even when it's not there.*

So we deliberately left off the other arm.

And this is something all writers must remember—what the reader knows should be there they'll supply *even when it's not*. Not only that, but that simple act of the reader supplying the essential last detail is what engages them, sucks them in, pins them down, makes them part of the story.

When we look at our favorite logos, our eye doesn't keep going back to them because it's found every single spec of information it needs. It goes back because there's something missing, and our eye knows what it is. Triumph! Over and over and over, we feel the satisfaction of supplying the missing piece. Over and over and over, there is the sense of completion, the instant of epiphany. *That's exactly right.*

Why?

Because that's what stories are—the unique, telling details that create the anchor points of our characters and plots, and everything in between the reader fills in from their own imagination.

We must focus on those unique, telling details. Make them as wonderful and vivid and telling as we possibly can. Then sit back and let the reader fill in the rest.

Have you ever wondered how the ancients got the constellations out of tiny handfuls of stars?

By reading them.

Drawing an Analogy

Applying the Analogy to Storytelling

So let's take the analogy between logo and storytelling the rest of the way.

She needed enough big dark elements to be recognizable at a casual glance...

This is our structure. We need a Hook, we need things to happen, and we need a Climax. And we need cause-and-effect leading inevitably from one event to the next. If we leave out any of these elements, we don't have a complete story.

But we can't use *everything*. There will always be mountains of notes, questions, interviews, cut scenes that nobody ever knows about but us. The entirety of our imaginary worlds? It will always be privately ours.

...but she also needed her itsy-bitsy little facial features to show up.

We also need supremely interesting characters for our protagonists. Who are they? What matters most in the world to them? How did they get into their predicaments, and how do they wish they could get out? They can't get out the way they want to—that's a given. The tension lies between what they *wish* they could do and what they actually *manage*.

They can't always get what they want. So they try and try and try until they get what they need.

We blacked in her hat and gloves...

This is establishing the anchor points of our structure. What is this story *about*? What's the Climax, the premise in a nutshell? And when did it start being about that, at the Hook? What's going to happen between the beginning and end of this story, how is the Climax's shadow going to fall backward over the characters as they struggle to make their way away from the Hook forging inevitably deeper into trouble, always heading toward that Climax? When our reader remembers this story, what will they remember?

A fascinating, uncontrollable couple love and need each other so deeply they destroy their lives fighting against the pressures that keep them separated until death brings them together forever.
 —*Wuthering Heights,* by Emily Bronte

A solitary seeker fascinated by an unfamiliar world traverses it until he learns what he needs to know.
 —*Stranger in a Strange Land,* Robert A. Heinlein

The members of a family torn apart by unexpected catastrophe reveal in their search for an explanation the terrible chasms between them all.
 —pretty much anything by Ivy Compton-Burnett

Addiction in tension. Fulfillment in resonance.

. . .(although the gloves have wonderful highlighted wrinkles in the soft leather). . .

This is where we choose our subplots. We know not everything can go in. But because we're writing a story and not designing a half-inch logo, we have room to layer in wonderful highlighted wrinkles, secondary issues, complications feeding always like the threads of a braid back into the main fuel driving our story through conflict.

Drawing an Analogy

...and exaggerated her features.

The protagonist *must* be the fullest, most powerful, most complex character. If we have a powerful secondary character, their relationship to the protagonist must take on a character of its own. Always remember that, as soon as we let a secondary character become more powerful and complex than our protagonist, our reader will jump ship for them. We must keep the basic needs that drive our protagonist palpitating.

We erased all of her from chin to gloves...

We lose a lot of our first draft when we tighten for structure and character development, especially if we pants. It's just the way it is. We set that stuff aside in its own folders and save it for another day.

...and then went back, meticulously re-creating only those lines absolutely necessary to give her definition.

And we will have pieces to add in revision, things we forgot to say or skipped over leaving only milemarkers to remind ourselves something goes there. It's fine. Stories are long. Novels—when we're writing them—are all but interminable. We won't force ourselves to slog through from beginning to end, all in elaborate detail, if it burns us out. We'll write it the way we want to, then go back and identify the holes and write those pieces. We'll meticulously re-create only those lines that are absolutely necessary.

She has a lot of ruffles around her face, which looked weird when they disappeared.

This kind of thing happens in revision. We delete things that aren't necessary, and it shows up other holes we hadn't seen before. Now we're making decisions about what goes into those holes. A tension-filled subplot? Brilliant, subtle illumination? Better, more vivid, more telling scenes always forcing the main plot forward?

We had to get just enough of them in to remove the weird without competing with her more important elements.

So we stay focused on where we're going and how we're going to get there. If some secondary character absolutely insists on being big, bright, and fascinating we can always set them aside for their own story. Nobody's limiting us to only this one.

The *pièce de résistance* turned out to be not even a part of her, but the shadow her cardboard cut-out cast on the wall when she was photographed.

And during the writing and revising and pondering and shaping of this story, we will find those elements that keep cropping up, the beautiful images and paradoxical character traits and significant telling details that make this story unique. They become symbolic. They turn into that subterranean layer of story running silent and deep beneath the plotline. They are the fuel for the final epiphany.

Then we looked at her other arm, which has no such line. We paused.

And when we get to the end of our Climax, we pause.

Drawing an Analogy

We were going to flip the line and use its opposite on the other side.

We re-think our notes on the Resolution, almost none of which we'll have taken before we started writing and most of which we'll have taken after we finished our early drafts.

. . .I remembered a fascinating fact about stylized images: what the eye knows should be there it will see *even when it's not there.*

We ask ourselves how much faith we have in the relationship between a writer and their reader—the magic of fiction, the power of epiphany—how much faith in this art and craft we love.

And we deliberately leave off the other arm.

Character is *Content*

Chapter 11

Being Mesmerized with Louisa May Alcott

Write what you love, not what you should

I think we're all agreed Laurie belonged with Jo.

I mean, why would an author *do* that? Marry Jo off to an elderly schoolteacher while sending her best friend into the arms of her preening, self-absorbed little sister? Laurie, the boy who accepts Jo as she is without preaching and loves her for her wit and strength and sense of adventure instead of in spite of them? Married off to the sister who's burned her *manuscripts*?

As it happens, Louisa May Alcott hated the preachiness of *Little Women* and her other popular novels. She wrote them for the money because, as she admitted, preaching does sell.

Her father, Bronson Alcott, was one of the Transcendentalists, the crowd to which Ralph Waldo Emerson and Henry David Thoreau belonged. It was only when her father gave talks on moral philosophy or taught in his revolutionary Temple School (where he raised a furor by teaching that procreation is linked to adults' inability to restrain themselves and which collapsed after white parents withdrew their children to protest the acceptance of a black child) that he ever made any money.

Alcott was raised in poverty not because her father—a highly-educated intellectual—was unable to support his family, but because work clashed with his philosophical doubts. Her mother, along with Louisa and her sisters, maintained them all on the communes to which Bronson took them, working incessantly to keep the family alive while Bronson met with his Transcendental pals to hash over the meaning of living.

For a few weeks in the fall of 1843 they even lived in a state of acute terror while Bronson actually pondered whether or not to abandon his wife and children to the poorhouse in order to pursue his philosophical destiny. The horror of that childhood experience must have stuck with Louisa for the rest of her life.

How would you get over such a trauma? What kind of *savoir-faire* would you have to *have*?

What that experience did, I believe, was split Louisa in half.

One half was still and would always be firmly in the grip of the social principles her parents and her father's friends expounded: the principles of self-sacrifice and living for what we owe humanity rather than what we deserve. It was adherence to these principles that led to both Alcott's fame as the author of some of the most heavily-peddled children's morality tales in the history of English literature and—unfortunately—her early death.

Alcott died of mercury poisoning from the medication she was given to cure the typhoid she contracted nursing casualties of the Civil War. She also, most likely, died of a combination of exhaustion and guilt, having throughout her final illness nursed her father in his while simultaneously raising her sister's orphaned daughter. When her father died, only two days before Alcott, he said to her, "Come with me."

Shades of Emily Bronte, who came down with a cold the day of her brother Branwell's funeral and died of the ensuing tuberculosis three months later.

However, the other half of Alcott was not the worshipful daughter of her father, the self-sacrificing child of her mother (her sister, Beth, died of the scarlet fever their mother brought home from her charitable works), the dutiful purveyor of morality to the young and impressionable. Before *Little Women* ever landed on a publisher's doorstep or fell into the hands of high-minded parents, Alcott had published a handful of stories in the pulp rags, the stories she herself loved, Jo's infamous "blood-and-thunder" tales.

I was given *Modern Magic: Five Stories* by Louisa May Alcott for my birthday one year and *A Modern Mephistopheles, and A Whisper in the Dark* the next.

Hot *dog*.

Here are stories worth reading! Magic shows, deception, opiates, hypnotism (known as mesmerism in Alcott's day). Friends venture unknowingly into danger under the influence of drugs, strangers lead each other astray, characters disappear and reappear under impossible circumstances. The dark, disturbing underbelly of human character blossoms with an unearthly light in Alcott's hands.

And the split between her two bodies of work—the harrowing self-sacrifice of the March sisters and the rambunctious exploration of the devil's domain—brought us both Laurie and his author's betrayal of him, both Amy's appalling vandalism and her saccharine reward.

Why did Alcott give Laurie to Amy? Because she thought she had to.

Why did she invent Laurie in the first place?

Because she *could*.

Don't waste your time trying to force your work into some popular fad. Alcott's done enough of that for all of us. If there's anything we can learn from her tortured boomerang between duty and passion it's that ulterior motive poisoned the well of genius from which Laurie and Jo were drawn.

Keep your well clean.

Chapter 12

Hunting the Ghost Tiger
Cause-&-effect

Taking the Tiger by the Tail

Let's talk about **premise**.

A friend and I decided one morning last winter I should write a ghost story for the holiday season, a sort of *Christmas Carol* where Scrooge turns out to be right.

We were whining on and on about how much we hate converting our living rooms into moldy indoor forests every year, with all the attendant branches poking us in the eye and greasy puddles and mountains of composting needles being ground into carpets with other things we don't normally leave underfoot. How frustrating it is to try to thread electric cords with little light bulbs through all of that, especially when we spend half an hour getting poked and prodded by the needles and branches and risking breaking the fragile little bulbs into a thousand cutting shards in the carpet, and then we're done and it turns out none of the bulbs work.

And hanging breakables from the wayward branches. Either climbing on teetering chairs to get a star on top of the tree and falling into the branches or putting a child up on our shoulders so *they* can fall into them. Our kids getting wound up on sugar from all the extra cookies and candycanes, so even if they don't fall into the tree we can enjoy the piercing, hysterical shrieks as they imagine they're just about to. The pointless fights among adults engendered by the raw nerves from listening to all the piercing shrieks. And getting to listen to nothing but Christmas carols for eight solid weeks.

Oh, yes. A ghost story.

So I thought right away, *What will be my Climax? My Development? My Hook?* And I had some ideas, which I had not yet written down, when I got deeply embroiled in sorting out the logic behind the story. Because ghost stories, being fantasy, need rules made up for them, and this involves a lot of **logic**.

It's bad enough to write a realistic story and let illogical things happen, but we simply can't get away with being illogical about fantasy. This is *deus ex machina* in the worst way, and as soon as the reader stops believing in our logic they stop caring about our story.

The real beauty of all stories is the logic behind them. Not only do we put our characters through hell, but we make sure the reader can't see *any way* to avoid it.

So I got involved in who the ghosts would be (I decided there'd be more than one), and why they were scroogey, and where, and when, and how. I sort of knew who the protagonist would be and how they'd get entangled with these ghosts, but then I had to get into the logic of how they'd get back *out* again. And that gave me a great Resolution. But it also gave me some problems with logic because, after all, if the Resolution is right there, why doesn't the protagonist just find it in the first place? I had good reasons for that, and they worked fabulously, but there were other loose threads in the logic, and that involved figuring out the logic behind *them*, and then making sure *that* didn't have loose threads, as well.

Guess what I was dealing with?

That's right. *Cause-&-effect.*

Someone does something. A full cause-&-effect action with a point. This is a story.

Hook: Why? What's the cause of this whole thing? This is known as the inciting incident—so named, I believe, by the screenwriting guru Robert McKee—and it's the first piece of the logic, the first *effect*, to sort out. When does this mess start? Why does it all happen? Why do these characters *do* this? Characters always have reasons for the things they do.

Backstory: And does that initial thing they do work out? Of course not. When it works out, the story ends. But why *doesn't* it work out? What's the logic behind the failure? The original reason this mess starts? The *cause* of that inciting incident? What logic can neither the characters nor the reader see?

Note that I did not say, "What information can neither the characters nor the reader see?" This is a *vital* distinction. We are not hiding things from the reader. That's trying to trick them, and 1) it very often doesn't work (don't aim for stupid readers), and 2) even when it does work, it's not fun for them.

We are *playing with logic.*

If I want ghosts in my story, naturally I must figure out why they're ghosts. What's my logic? They're ghosts for a reason. That reason is intricately tied to what's going to happen to my protagonist.

My premise—my logic—is the point of my whole story.

The three ghosts of Christmas exist for the purpose of teaching a grouchy old fart why kindness matters.
  —*A Christmas Carol,* Charles Dickens

The ghosts of the governess and her paramour exist to illuminate what's happened to the two children.
—"The Turn of the Screw," Henry James

The poltergeist exists to frighten the girl and her mother for the entertainment of her dreadful father.
— *The Fountain Overflows*, Rebecca West

effect: ghosts
cause: logic

Now we can see that the original logic, which I've come up with after I decided what I want in my story, actually begins *before* my story. That makes it (I know you know this) Backstory. How my characters got into this mess has everything to do with what the mess is and how it's going to blow up in their faces. It's all tied together.

So once I'm at the root of the Backstory (who are these ghosts and why?), I have the tiger by the tail, and I can work my way forward through my story hand-over-hand, following the cause-&-effect:

If these characters became ghosts for this original reason

And if this protagonist gets entangled with them for that Hook reason

Then what happens?

That 'then what' is the effect of the Backstory mixed with the inciting incident: my Hook.

And how does the protagonist react to that effect? How do the ghosts react? The other characters? That's what the reader wants to know.

The Art & Craft of Story

And what does that reaction cause? Another effect. The characters have made decisions, taken action, tried to extricate themselves from their problem—and failed. To which, again, everyone must react.

And what does that reaction cause that?

And that? And that? And that?

Hand-over-hand, up the tiger's body from the tip of the tail all the way to the other end, where my protagonist must, with impeccable logic, stick their head into the tiger's mouth.

What's going to make them do that? The accumulation of logic all the way.

Now, granted, by the time they've worked their way hand-over-hand all the way up a tiger's body, my protagonist should reasonably know better than to stick their head into its mouth. So there must be something way, way back there on the tip of the tiger's tail that makes this inevitable. I might not know what it is before I get to the tiger's head the first time. That's okay. That's the glory and wonder of fiction—I get to go back and add things later, and the reader never finds out.

From the tiger's head, I look back over the entire chain of events I've followed, and the logic is perfect, the cause-&-effect is unbeatable. It's all set.

Now I look at that lolling tongue and those Bowie-knife teeth, and I need a *really good reason* for my protagonist to go for it.

I review my logic. What's been driving these characters this whole way? It doesn't matter if I didn't plan it out in detail. Now that I've gotten them here, I can stretch and yawn and scratch my belly and just generally take my time figuring it out. *No one will ever know.*

I notice something running like a thread through the story, and it has to do with my protagonist's character, their one

Hunting the Ghost Tiger

driving need, how they're forced to react to things in one way and one way only. It's just who they are. It's their reason for being.

What can this golden, essential reason for being possibly have to do with sticking their head in the tiger's mouth? There must be oodles of logical possibilities. The important thing is that this protagonist is *driven*. Something has made them do the things they've done. That same something is going to make them take this one, last, gigantically disastrous step.

What's the logic? I must have *some* reason for telling this story. And it's my job to discover what it is.

Then I go back to the beginning of my story and *plant a clue* to that reason in the inciting incident.

So we can see how that particular Hook, following the unshakeable logic of the Backstory, leads my protagonist by the logic of cause-&-effect all the way through the Development *inevitably* to the Climax, the whole reason I'm telling this story. The illumination of my original premise.

Where I let the tiger eat them.

And they turn into a ghost!

Focusing the Tiger

I've dumped things quite unceremoniously on the casual question, "What's the logic?" As in, "It's lying right there! Come on—pick it *up!*"

But what if it's not lying right there in front of me? What if I've looked everywhere, gotten down and crawled around on my hands and knees searching with a magnifying glass, looked under every rock and in every cranny, and still not found it? What if I am, in fact, sitting at my desk this very minute contemplating a premise, a series of Conflicts, and a tiger's mouth, and my characters are standing back shaking their heads solemnly and pointing in my general direction: "*You* do it"?

My characters are too smart for me.

So let's talk about endings. Lolling tongues and Bowie-knife teeth. Prying open those jaws and inserting the cranium.

I tell writers: identify your protagonist and their greatest need, then from that identify their worst nightmare, which always involves *not being able to meet* of their greatest need.

That's the Climax.

But there's a little more to it than that, because the *reason* a protagonist can't meet their greatest need is that they have a *second equally-great* need, and the two needs are in mutually-exclusive conflict with each other. (This should be sounding very familiar!)

The need to obey his great-uncle's deathbed command to carry religion to the secular conflicts with the need to escape his great-uncle's religious fanaticism.
    —Francis Tarwater in *The Violent Bear It Away*, Flannery O'Connor

The need to find spiritual fulfillment in a small African tribe conflicts with the need to save his skin from the tribal leaders.
    —Eugene Henderson in *Henderson the Rain King*, Saul Bellow

The need to hold onto their family traditions and live their daily lives conflicts with the need to cope with Ireland's violent attempts to overthrow British dominance.
    —the Naylor family in *The Last September*, Elizabeth Bowen

And there of course is Henry James' narrator's need to acquire the precious "Aspern Papers," which conflicts with his need to avoid marrying a woman he does not love.

My characters have a very good reason to explore this particular tiger. They *need to*.

They also have a very good reason to *fight against* this tiger. The tiger does not come to them easily at all!

And the conflict between these two needs both blinds them and drives them relentlessly forward.

So by the time they get to the tiger's head, they've spent the entire story besting the odds in order to *hang onto* this darn tiger, blind to the inherent danger of such a plan. They've put their identity, their welfare, their very lives on the line for the sake of it. This tiger has become everything they want out of living. So sticking their heads in its mouth is the only logical (get that—logical!) culmination of this devotion.

It is the actual process of going hand-over-hand up the tiger's body that ingrains the need for this culmination in them so powerfully.

This is why I tell writers not to write the Climax until they've written the entire novel. Because the tiger's mouth is created out of the tiger's body. As we write chapters, episodes, scenes about these characters—moving them inexorably from their Hook to their dreadful Climax—we are creating the pressures that force the characters eventually to stick their heads in that tiger's mouth.

What happens to the protagonist in the Hook? Something impacts on them. Just as in life, what happens to someone changes them in some way—it either counters or reinforces a previous disposition, it creates a little bit more extremity in an already-weakened area, it heightens the contrast between their highs and lows. It, in fact, adds tension.

Now we figure out how the Hook leads to the first Conflict. How can that and the succeeding Conflicts continue to deepen the grooves, intensify the peaks, of this character's experience? How does the protagonist's overwhelming need for first one thing and then the other force them again and again into situations—Conflicts—in which those grooves and peaks become worse and worse?

How does the geography of the tiger's body eventually create the shape of the mouth the protagonist *can no longer* get out of?

It is the conflict between a protagonist's two needs that creates their experience of the tiger's body.

And the body of the tiger is our story.

Chapter 13

Developing Character
A multi-chambered heart

Differentiating Yourself from Your Reader

We already know we, as human beings, love stories because they teach us how to live. In particular, they teach us how to cope with the inevitable 'slings and arrows of outrageous fortune,' how to duck when we've got to duck, how to take it when we're not quick enough to duck, and what to do after we have failed to duck.

What's the point of learning how to live easy? We're pretty sure we can fly *that* one by the seat of our pants.

So one of the biggest problems facing aspiring writers is differentiating between themselves and their creations.

The thing is, we *love* these characters. That's why we create them. We thrill to their outlook, we're heartbroken over their problems, we laugh our heads off at their jokes. We cherish them, we admire them, we identify with them.

How many first-person novels have we ever read in critique workshops where the protagonist has a blank personality? That's because the writer's not writing about a character, they're writing about themself. And, in their mind,

Developing Character

they're not just another human personality—they're *the* human personality. Beyond characterization.

It is so easy to assume everyone lives in our heads with us.

When I was a teenager, my father announced over dinner one night he'd just read *Alice Through the Looking-Glass* and realized he might be the White King.

"Maybe I'm dreaming all of you," he said. "How would you know?"

"Maybe *I'm* dreaming *you*." I was fifteen, a master of logic, and didn't care who knew it. "How would *you* know?"

We don't dream our readers. Not the ones we hope will read us someday, anyway. We do have to differentiate between ourselves, our readers, and our characters, and we have to differentiate between the individual characters, as well. *And* we have to differentiate between how our characters act when they're taking a breather and how they act when they're cowering under a hailstorm of dreadful, stinking, atrocious bad luck.

But here's the good news! We don't have to put our characters through a James Bondish ticking-bomb moment to give them conflict. What readers like more than anything else is when the conflict is *internal*.

Why?

What could readers possibly get out of seeing other people—even imaginary people—go through awful internal turmoil, fighting themselves, losing to themselves, defeating themselves, triumphing over themselves, transcending the reality of *being* themselves? Just like we do ourselves?

Fiction is revealing the unknowable, saying the unsayable. And the unsayable we all live with is: *it hurts to be us*.

Buddha knew this. He lived a cushy life for a long time, wandered off one day to sit under a tree and not eat until he figured out the meaning of it all, and came back saying, "Life is suffering. Knock off the funny stuff, you guys."

Great philosopher though he was, he was no fiction writer. He would never have put characters into trouble on purpose. But he understood something we all need to understand: characters are born to suffer.

When we look for ways to give our characters conflict, we must not be inhibited by our Buddha nature. Our characters are not us. They're not even *real*.

But, at the same time, we must not forget our Buddha nature. Our *readers* are real. And they desperately need to learn how to suffer with grace.

One night over the dinner table my father said to my mother, "I've got you trained."

She laughed. "I've got *you* trained."

I looked at my little sister. "We've got them trained."

Everybody thinks they're the White King.

But who is it *really*?

Seeing What Your Reader Sees in Character

We can't write publishable books solely for ourselves. This is the bedrock of what I know about fiction: "It's not about the writer's experience, it's about the *reader's*."

If it was only about the writer's experience, we'd just write it and then keep it around for the rest of our lives, re-reading it whenever we got the wind up, wouldn't we? And that's not what some of us have in mind, is it?

Okay, I actually *do* do that. However, the writing we want to be read by *other people*—by readers—we have to write for them. We don't buy our kids clothes to fit ourselves.

And what the reader wants is to read about people like them. They want to be able to identify with our characters, to feel in their bones, *This character is* me. *Oh, this is the story of my life!*

So we have to be able to create characters that speak for the reader. And to do that, we must understand how the reader experiences life.

1. Our reader's internal world is confusing

We're all masses of seething anguish and obfuscation. Being a storyteller means having empathy for the human condition.

Giving our reader concrete, identifiable guideposts to what's going on inside our characters helps the reader sort out their own internal world. A *lot*. It helps them get into our story, and it helps them to stay there.

Help the reader simplify themself.

What kinds of concrete guideposts can we give a reader?

- The poles of our character's extremes: how are they fun to be around? How are they not so fun? What are they like when they're happy? What about when they're not so happy? What are they like when they get what they want? And what about when they don't?
- A set number of challenges our characters have to face: what annoys them? What hurts them? What breaks their hearts? And then, just when they think they've survived the worst, what totally wrecks their lives?
- An alternating pattern between types of event: when are they fired up? When are they relieved? When do they gird their loins? When are they hoisted on their own petard? How can we keep yanking their nose

rings back and forth, right and left, up and down, through every single page?

2. Our reader's external world is also confusing

Stuff is always coming at them they don't expect or, if they do, they dread. Friends get snippy, co-workers cheat on workloads, relatives lay guilt trips, children and partners are yoked to the eyeballs on seriously important needs.

Give the reader ways to categorize the insanity.

How can we do this?

- Simplify our characters' dilemmas. Don't send them bumbling aimlessly through the world exactly the way real people do, meeting infinite strangers and keeping track of numerous almost-identical friends and remembering who went where with whom that time they didn't accomplish whatever. Condense multiple characters into one whenever possible. Shape their conflicts toward the obvious high points. Don't make pointless detours. Don't trick.
- Focus our characters' progress. We all take two steps forward and one step back. But we also take about a zillion steps sideways, this way and that, for no particular reason at all. We must give our characters at least two conflicting needs that cause certain behaviors that have effects and make our characters follow those conflicting needs through those effects into further causes and further effects. It's not the way we live, but it helps life make sense to portray it that way. Just two conflicting needs are plenty. Three if we're real wild things.

3. Our reader's life is boring

They work for a living. They have responsibilities. Even when they're lying on a beach in Bali listening to the soft *shoof* of the waves on sand and the papery rustle of palm leaves in a salty breeze, they're wondering how they're going to get through another Thanksgiving with their closest kin, sitting around burping and farting and watching reality TV. They're cringing from the thought of getting on that plane and winding up, this exact time two weeks from today, in the same ole squeaky chair in the same ole veal-fattening pen. The endless drudgery is always in the back of their mind.

Relieve the reader's suffering.

What can we do to liven things up for them?

- Give our characters fascinating personality traits. Don't make them happy to sit around the kitchen stuffing envelopes for a hundred pages. Don't put them on the phone talking in whiny voices about the same uninteresting thing over and over again. Don't make them *dull*. We may not be the most charismatic things coming down the pike—but we must make every protagonist one.
- Let exciting things happen to our characters. Don't write about the boring parts of their lives. They brush their teeth, wash the dishes, yell at their kids to clean their rooms. Yeah, yeah, our reader knows. They do that too. You know what? They're largely on autopilot while they're doing it for *real people* they *really love*. They won't bother wading through it for imaginary people nobody actually loves but us. Stick to the scenes, the very moments, when Important Things Happen.

- Give our reader room to have thoughts of their own. Don't explain every single thing that passes through our characters' brains. Don't point out foreshadowing or get melodramatic over what happens to our characters or—god forbid—put information into their mouths the reader *already knows*. Have a sense of personal space.

Finally—

4. Our reader looks up to us

They really do. If they didn't, they wouldn't be reading our story. Strive to create realistic, breathing, complex, believable characters for them to meet and be fascinated by and devote hard-won hours of their precious time to.

We have a professional responsibility to our reader.

Live up to it.

Understanding Sympathetic Character

The most important thing we need to do when we create a protagonist is make them someone the reader absolutely *loves* traveling all the way up the tiger alongside. This is not an easy trip, it's not always a pleasant trip, and it can at times be quite a harrowing trip (if we do it right). So this protagonist must be *intensely sympathetic* to our reader.

But what does that really mean to storytelling, 'sympathetic' and 'unsympathetic' characters?

Unsympathetic characters can be summed up in one word: boring.

Boring?

Boring.

Developing Character

But what about the evil arch-nemesis of the wonderful heroine? What about the wicked wizard/psychopathic stalker/heartless boss/reckless abuser/cruel shoe-seller who forces the struggling hero to run a mile in tight shoes? What about the monster the protagonist has to defeat in the spectacular, death-defying Climax, which monster must be described in only the most horrific and disgusting terms so the reader will cheer when the protagonist finally makes it *pay*?

Boring. One-dimensional characters having nothing to say, nothing to show the reader, no reason for them to read the words of which they consist.

Ultimate fictional evil? No. Real evil happens in the real world. It is rooted in humanity, and because it is rooted in humanity it is complex. One-dimensional bogeys aren't evil. Why would we waste our precious moments on this planet trying to figure out, "I wonder what I can write to make my reader vomit all over my book"? We don't know. Do you know why? Because we're not evil.

Never put anything in your fiction that is not true to you.

Two-dimensional characters are almost as bad. The staid, ignorant, housewife-slash-unpleasant mother. The dull, plodding, workaholic father. The girlfriend who suckers the hero into bed and turns into a gold-digging shrew. The boyfriend who lies about love and laughs cruelly when the heroine cries. The bullying authority figure. The cringing wimp. The featureless, characterless, mindless wives and husbands and children and siblings and neighbors (especially neighbors, for some reason) populating the worlds through which protagonists only marginally less white-washed make their hapless ways. Even the anti-hero who's just so troubled and jaded and tough they *have* to hide their third dimension under an impenetrable exterior of ignorance & apathy. ("I don't know, and I don't care.")

Hear that clunk? That's the reader's head hitting the desk.

But what about one- and two-dimensional *sympathetic* characters?

They don't exist.

Not even the muscle-bound hunk who sweeps the heroine off her feet? The good-hearted best friend? The wise elderly teacher/smart-alec sidekick/sweet sibling/breathless admirer? The people who surround the protagonist demonstrating for the reader exactly how they're supposed to see them?

I'm afraid that's not sympathetic. That's transparent machination. Readers don't like machination, they like characters who are honestly intriguing.

Sympathetic characters are *always* three-dimensional characters. Characters with *internal conflict*.

But how can we lump all three-dimensional characters together under the heading 'sympathetic'? That can't be true. Heathcliff and Catherine aren't 'sympathetic.'

Oh, but they are! Torn between their passion for each other, for their beloved moors, for the wild things with which they identify, and their uncontrollable fury and fascination with the financial and social constraints of human society? Readers *love* those two, best-selling and going strong even after a hundred and fifty years.

Or Kurtz—with his anguished, "the horror! the horror!"—what about him?

Intensely sympathetic! Not only has he created his own nightmare, he's human enough to discover what he's done and react to the knowledge, in the final hour, in all his soul-wracking turmoil.

Developing Character

Fyodor Pavlovich Karamazov, the drunken, abusive father of the brothers who struggled so desperately, in their separate ways, to come to terms with his death?

Oh, Dostoevsky was a master. He couldn't write a less-than-three-dimensional character to save his *life*.

A sympathetic character, by definition, is one with whom the reader feels some level of sympathy. One with whom the reader, in some way, identifies.

You know that old saw about villains who steal the show? Those are sympathetic characters.

So now we see something mesmerizing, and that is that a sympathetic character is *always* a three-dimensional character, and a three-dimensional character is *always* one with powerfully conflicting facets to their personality. A sympathetic character is both an angel and a devil. A sympathetic character is one whom the reader both loves and hates, both admires and yells, "Oh, no!" over, a character who—here it comes—both pushes the reader away and pulls them back again. Push/pull. Push/pull.

Heathcliff, when he's young, is a teased and tormented hothead who takes his lumps with grace (he lets Hindley hit him in the chest with an *anvil* in exchange for Hindley's pony—*ow!*) and—unlike the spoiled kids around him—never complains once when they all come down with a deadly childhood disease. Even as a bitter, vindictive man, the last illness of his one beloved can bring him to stand under a tree outside her window all night while she raves with brain fever, oblivious to his presence, oblivious to him bashing his head against the tree trunk in agony until he bleeds. When he gets the chance to see her, does he play the cold, vicious bastard he's so famous for? No—he grasps her in his arms and kisses her frantically all over her face and hands. He begs her to live. He breaks down in tears.

He becomes *human*.

Once on Twitter I had a brief but spirited disagreement with someone in which they informed me that Indiana Jones would kick Han Solo's butt.

"So not possible," I said.

"Sorry to be the one to tell you," they said.

"Han's younger," I said.

Why do we even *care*?

Because Harrison Ford has that lovable jerk persona down to a science: a character who's both callous and tender, both vulnerable and tough as nails, both commando and confused. ("It was nothing. Everything's fine. We're all fine here, don't come check — ah — how are *you*?")

A sympathetic character has all those types of wonderful characteristics we hope we have when we're on top of the world, the strength and charm and wit and charisma, completely mixed in with all those dreadful characteristics we actually know we have when the chips are down, the fear and self-doubt and terrible propensity to make really, incredibly wrong mistakes. Do you know why they're sympathetic?

Because they're *us*.

We must use this to our advantage. Don't waste time trying to create The Most Dreadful Dastardly Criminal Ever or The Greatest Hero/Lover/Genius.

Nobody caaaaaaaaares.

Create sympathetic characters. Create real people.

Chapter 14

Condensing & Contrasting Characters
Two sides to a single coin

Condensing Multiple Characters into One

Is your manuscript crawling with miscellaneous people?

Marcel Proust supposedly put over 2,000 characters into *Remembrance of Things Past*. And even for seven volumes — *that's a lot of characters.*

Don't do this. Proust was creating characters out of people he'd really known, rambling on rather indiscriminately about moments, impressions, passing ideas as if he had all the time in the world — which, in fact, he did. He was bed-ridden at the end of his life with debilitating asthma, and writing his single, unending novel was the only thing going on with him. He was a brilliant, detail-obsessed author simply *overloaded* with free time.

But our readers don't have the attention span to keep track of over 2,000 characters. In fact, they prefer less than twenty. In fact, they're most riveted if we can keep it down to a half-dozen. Or two. Maybe one.

Condensing & Contrasting Characters

Can we write an entire novel about only one person? Hey, we can try!

I recommend less than ten. One or two protagonists. (Ensemble casts work better on the screen than they do in novels, although if we're really talented and really dedicated and really determined, we could probably do something powerful.) Two to six secondary characters.

That's all the significant figures.

And a handful of minor supporting characters. Don't litter the place up with miscellaneous co-workers and police officers and almost-identical family members. Even our minor supporting characters must have *character*.

Do we have three characters when two or even one would do? Explore the possibilities of condensing their personalities down into one. Then consider what happens when we lump three people's problems onto one person's head. Spend some time doodling links between the characters on a sheet of paper.

Tap your chin and ask yourself, "If I make Melvin the detective instead of Howie, how does that affect his love affair with Edna Jean, the State Senator? If I give Melvin his friend Lawrence's bad divorce and custody problems, what kind of pressure will that put on him to follow up clues even faster and more effectively? And when the gun-runner's plane crashes on take-off from Edna Jean's country estate, doesn't that eliminate the whole business about Melvin getting the message to Howie, while forcing him to deal with his kids in the process of dashing to the crash site before the gun-runner gets into her disguise as Edna Jean's mute cousin Natasha?"

You see how condensing characters ratchets the tension, while upping the ante on whoever's left? Simplify, simplify, simplify. This is how we create layers: by accordioning the surface into deeper and vastly more tightly-knitted complexity.

Condensing Characters for Internal Conflict

Now let's talk about what effect condensing multiple characters has on a protagonist.

I once wrote a novel based loosely on the coffee shop where I worked. We poor misfits of a staff comprised a truly stunning spectrum of the socially-impaired, and the coffee shop was run—for a time at least—on the principles of the manager's therapy. She thought maybe if we just asked nicely enough the clientele might be prevailed upon to handle the business of buying from us without our intervention. At that point it seemed like only a short step from reality to fantasy, so I took it.

And it was *fabulous*.

There I was, pantsing merrily along. (We didn't have the word pantsing in those days. We called it writing "off the top of your head." It was probably only a lucky glitch in the Matrix that we don't all call it now "heading" or, even worse, "topping.") Here came a character, a big, loud, domineering guy based more or less on a beloved uncle and more or less on the grouch in management at the coffee shop. And here came another character, a gentle, sensitive guy based more or less on my college mentor and more or less on the peacemaker in management. I thought it would be lovely if these guys were close friends, although in real life they weren't.

And it was.

So I kept writing, throwing in characters wherever they seemed appropriate and watching what happened when they interacted. All such glorious fun!

But then I took my fledgling novel to the Community of Writers at Squaw Valley, and one of the things critiquers said was, "You know, you've got a *lot* of characters." And it was

Condensing & Contrasting Characters

true. You couldn't even tell whom the story was about. (I *still* have trouble keeping it straight whom that story is about.)

Anne Lamott told me, in all kindness—she's a very kind person—"You have written this wonderful story, this Michelangelo's David, kind of buried behind all its hair. But you need to decide who it's about and gently clear the hair from its face."

So I went home, armed with the kindness of the author of a great (then-new) book on writing, and began thinking about how to clear the hair from its face. And, as I did, I began condensing characters.

Did those two friends—true-to-life as it was to give that dinky café more managers than the Ritz—absolutely *have* to be two different people? Could this place have only one manager, the man who loves, cares for, rails against, and survives the plot alongside the one main tragic character, the café's lesbian owner? What would that do to the story?

Well, it would focus it more on the relationship between the manager and owner. By removing the relationship between the two managers and letting the relationship between the manager and owner stand alone, it clarified the major theme of the novel, which is what happens to a lifelong love at the end of that life. (My grandmother had just died and left my grandfather completely bereft, and I had promised her on her deathbed to watch over him, so I was spending a lot of my weekends with him and witnessing the indescribable heartache that waits at the end of a long and happy marriage.)

It would streamline the Backstory from a trivial secondary plotline between these two managers—who, in the first version, apparently met thirty years earlier in passing and only came together later through a second fortuitous accidental meeting—into the essential information about how this manager and owner came to be in this café going through their drama now.

And even more than all that, it would multiply the facets of that manager's personality, so that he'd become not only loud and domineering but also sensitive and caring, not only overbearing and with a voice he could use to wake the dead, but profoundly wounded, lost and afraid among his own demons, fighting tooth-&-nail his own imminent collapse.

It would give him enormous *internal conflict*.

And through his enormous internal conflict, I found what holds him and the café owner together, the deeper layers between them, the unspoken ties that have given them this lifelong unfulfilled love—the fact that she's lesbian is the fuel for the entire plot—as well as the tragedy they're facing in this particular story.

Condensing him made both him and their story *real*.

I'll tell you who pointed me into the wind with this: Lucia Orth, author of the critically-acclaimed novel *Baby Jesus Pawn Shop*. She was working on an early draft of her novel at the time, so we were critiquing each other's manuscripts, and she said, "Is he in love with her?" I said, "Oh, no. She's gay. They're just friends." And Lucia said, "Because *that* I would find riveting—*unrequited love*."

And of course she was absolutely right.

Condensing Characters for Contrast

One of the most important things about character is opposition. They must be in opposition to each other, they must be in opposition to their story, they must be in opposition to themself.

Condensing & Contrasting Characters

I'm one of three sisters very close in age. We have a lot of *similarities*. So if I were writing a novel in which the interplay between us was only a minor element, I'd shrink us down to one. We don't have enough contrast in our basic personalities.

Of course, I'd shrink us down to *me*.

Even worse were my grandmother's parents, one from a family of twelve and the other from a family of fourteen. Between them they had *twenty-four siblings*. You should see the family photos.

If we wanted to put a family that size into a novel, we'd have no choice but to make it about *being* a family of that size. We couldn't possibly create twenty-four people of sufficient contrast. And we couldn't have all those extras wandering around without a really compelling reason.

Contrast: the basic quality that makes characters visible to the reader.

Say we've got a couple of nice, normal people for our heroine and hero. A pair of charming ducks. But we can't just *leave* them a pair of charming ducks. They've got to contrast to each other. They've got to exemplify, somehow, the basic, fundamental differences between all individual human beings.

This is why readers like heroes and villains. It's easy math.

So we want to set up a dichotomy between these two characters, which of course turns out to be the root of all their ills.

They're super-compatible. They both love art and basketball and city life and role-playing bizarre games in front of other people. They love their life. They love each other. All's well in their world.

But there's an abyss between them, and it's the abyss that's going to eventually tear them apart.

Say when she was young she accidentally shot her brother while hunting and now has terrible recurring dreams about it. At the same time, he's a Licensed Practical Nurse and works in the ER. That contrast between their characters is going to bring about their worst nightmare, because when he's in charge of the ER the night a gunshot victim is brought in who rises unexpectedly from the gurney and pulls a pistol from the back of their belt and begins picking off staff, she's the only person who can drag him to safety and follow his gasped instructions on digging out the bullet so she can save his life...

Or.

He's secretly gay. And she's secretly lesbian. But they have to have a child (why? who knows? maybe they're aristocrats of the Edwardian era and need an heir, like Vita Sackville-West and Harold Nicholson). And the fact that they're terrified of revealing their secrets to anyone—especially each other—ratchets the tension on their contrast sky-high and means their efforts to live up to the pressures upon them result in either great comedy or great tragedy, depending upon the tone we want to take...

Or.

They're not really a couple. But they have to *pretend* to be a couple for very urgent reasons. Maybe they're in a Witness Protection Program. And their lives depend upon them maintaining the fiction of their cover. And during the course of the story it turns out one of them isn't really a witness, which is, naturally, the contrast between them. And that means the other *isn't really protected*...

Do you see how the contrast between characters is the fuel that makes our story a great, big paintball aimed right at the reader's head?

Now try condensing some of these characters.

Condensing & Contrasting Characters

Say the woman who accidentally shot her brother originally had two sisters. They aren't identical—no two of us are identical—but the sisters don't really have a good reason to be there besides the fact that we have a lot of characteristics we want to use. We want a social climber, a tomboy, a Mommy's Little Girl. We want someone who'll knock others down to get her way, a black sheep, and someone with a (slightly-strained) smile for every season. We have all this stuff going on, and we need someone to paste it onto.

But what if we eliminate the sisters? (They aren't any use, anyway—it's not as though she has more than surface conversations with them and those not essential to the plot.) What if we give *all those characteristics* to the same character?

Or maybe the homosexual man originally had a straight best friend with all the qualities we didn't know how to give our effeminate gay blade. The best friend is big, muscular, athletic, and has a way with the ladies. We've made our gay blade thin, willowy, soft-voiced, and limp-wristed.

What happens if we combine the two? Make the gay man big, willowy, muscular, soft-voiced, supremely athletic, with a charming way with the ladies to hide his passion for their boyfriends and brothers? The ladies don't mind his limp wrist. They think he's being sophisticated.

And the lesbian woman—maybe she originally was bluff and hearty, with a fondness for fresh air and dogs and comfortable shoes. (Do you know the old Robin Williams definition of lesbians? Women wearing comfortable shoes.) And maybe the social-climber sister was intensely competitive, while the smiley sister was a fainting lily who spent a lot of time on her chaise longue sipping absinthe and reading Lord Byron and fluttering her eyelashes at the big charming dude with muscles.

What if we made the lesbian a delicate flower with a fondness for fresh air and dogs and comfortable shoes, whose intense competitiveness makes her constantly over-do the bluff and hearty and have to retreat to her chaise longue with Lord Byron, while her husband brings her absinthe with a limp wrist and she flutters her eyelashes at him hoping against hope he hasn't seen her rolling in the hay with the neighbor's governess?

And after they've survived the shoot-out in ER, he has to testify against the perpetrator, who can identify him. So he's put into a Witness Protection Program and given a fake wife, with whom our heroine falls in love...

Do you see how giving our characters powerful internal conflict brings them vividly alive? It forces us to climb over the obstacle course of our unconscious assumptions and clichés and create unique people with real needs and desires, real gestures and mannerisms, even while keeping them focused on their conflicted driving needs that get them (you saw this coming) from Hook, through Development, all the way to the Climax.

Which is now about a zillion times more interesting and compelling, since we've given ourselves so much richer and more *substantial* material to work with.

Chapter 15

Using Character
The jaws of life

Using Character to Create Plot

Has anyone ever told you, "plot grows out of character"? Well, I happen to know they have. *I've* said it.

But what do we *mean*?

We mean: character is the alpha and omega of fiction. And characters are only important to readers insofar as they *need* things. Things that contrast. Things that conflict. When someone seriously, desperately, aggressively *needs* two mutually-exclusive things, well, stuff tends to happen to them. Big, exciting stuff! That's the fabulous stuff of fiction.

One afternoon on Twitter I started a conversation I called, for no particular reason, #editingchat. A few readers and I conducted a little experiment in which we demonstrated Developmental Editing on an unwritten story. I said, "Someone give me a story in a sentence," and someone gave us three aspects of a story: a death, a birth, and a mission, the protagonist a woman.

So I said, "What does this woman *need*?" And I opened it up to everyone—we were just horsing around.

Using Character

It turned out what this woman needs is forgiveness for a death due to the mission, specifically the death of the father of her baby. Somehow, she's done something that makes her think she's guilty, that she needs to stick with the mission in order to redeem his death, to prove to herself and others he has not died in vain. To earn forgiveness.

Then I said, "What *else* does she need? What *prevents her* from completely fulfilling her original need right now?"

And it turned out she also needs to survive—in particular she needs her baby to survive.

So we talked for a long time about what kind of situation could force that woman to choose between earning forgiveness and protecting her baby. We got a lot of ideas about what choice she should make—to give up seeking forgiveness outside herself, to realize her beloved died for her sake, to learn she can only get true forgiveness from herself.

"You are some optimistic little chipmunks, aren't you?" I said. "You really want to skip the Climax and get straight to that Resolution, don't you?"

In this way we learned what motivates a reader to read an entire story: *wanting to know the Resolution*.

But we don't know the Resolution before we finish writing our story. What we need to discover first is the Climax.

So we went back to it: what situation could force this woman to choose between her loyalty to her dead beloved—that fierce need to redeem his death, to earn forgiveness for what she cannot undo—and her instinct to protect her baby.

"What if the baby were in danger?" the writer suggested.

Well, that's a pretty good headlock to get that protagonist in! She's working on this mission that means everything in the world to her, but suddenly her baby's in danger and she has to choose between continuing her mission and saving her baby's life.

And that's when we learned that needs must reside not only in the protagonist (and their writer), but, most essentially, inside *the reader*.

Because we all know we have to save babies' lives! That's a top priority instilled in nearly all of us at a very early age. Those of us who don't have it...well, we're not generally interested in fiction. We can't empathize with humanity in general, and empathy is one of those things that fiction is about *in spades*.

So if we just make this protagonist choose between saving her baby and continuing her so-far hopeless pursuit of forgiveness through a mission that may or may not mean much to the reader, the reader's going to close the book with a satisfying snap and say, "All done! Conflict resolved."

This is the great, vast luxury of fiction. Because creating a *need for forgiveness* in our reader as powerful as their *need to save babies' lives* is what this story is all about.

Write it—the story of how this one character, this realistic, three-dimensional, internally-conflicted woman, becomes more and more deeply enmeshed in this mission, with her dreadful, transcendental need to prove her beloved did not die in vain. Give her a series of catastrophes as the mission progresses, earthshaking developments to put the reader on the edge of their seat. Make her engagement with this mission, her pursuit of forgiveness, as detailed and real and vivid as humanly possible.

At the same time, bring in the baby, but keep it secondary to the main plot (undercut the reader's natural investment in saving babies). Let her pregnancy be a subplot running through the story of the mission. Let her get pregnant (or discover her pregnancy), let her suffer a major setback in her pregnancy, let her give birth under terrible, almost deadly circumstances, and then, for a short time at least, let her believe everything's finally going to be all right. She made it. She's almost there, with both forgiveness and child safe. That's the Faux Resolution.

Then when we put the baby in danger and bring the woman all the way to the brink of her nightmare, where she must choose between forgiveness and child, we've got our reader exactly where our protagonist is: trapped between inescapable choices, forced to face themselves in their darkest and, maybe, brightest hour, tormented by the sheer reality of existence.

Which is where epiphany lies.

Using Character to Fuel Momentum

Every day, in every way, I am always telling aspiring writers, "Whatever you do, *never* interfere with the forward motion of your plot." Life is short, and stories are legion. We haven't got that kind of time.

But even better than simply not interfering, we need to know how to *increase* that forward motion.

Momentum: from snowball to avalanche.

We've been talking about how to use character to create plot, how our protagonist's two conflicting *needs* create the nightmare collision that is their inevitable Climax. But, while we're exploring this plot, how do we go beyond the admonishment not to interfere with our plot's momentum and actually increase the momentum, exaggerate, *fuel* it? Through character?

By taking every opportunity to conflict those two needs. And, at carefully timed intervals, *increase them*.

This technique is rooted in the character's freedom of choice. Because every time we set up a decision for them—**A** or **B**—whatever they choose leads to **C**, which we must arrange to be even worse than whatever they *didn't* choose.

Say a man *needs* to be safely on the right side of the law, even to believe in justice, or at least not make things any worse for himself. He's in prison for a crime he didn't commit, and he has a health problem the prison environment is exacerbating badly. Staying and sticking out his term keeps him safe from further prosecution. But he also *needs* to survive.

He needs:

1) to be safe from the law (which he knows now he won't necessarily be even if he avoids breaking it)
2) to live

His choices are:

A: *obediently stick out his term and hope prison doesn't kill him,* or
B: *break out of prison and safeguard his health*

He chooses a need, and he breaks out of San Quentin.

Now, the movie version of David Goodis' *noir* classic, *Dark Passage*, made film history for the most inadvertently hilarious introductory scenes ever: the camera acting as the eyes of the protagonist, Humphrey Bogart, who must, upon his escape from prison, have plastic surgery to make his face unrecognizable. (They pulled this camera stunt so they wouldn't have to either use another actor or attempt to alter beyond recognition Bogey himself. It apparently did not occur to anyone that if we were going to have plastic surgery, we

Using Character

might question making ourselves look like Humphrey Bogart. Charming, yes. Powerful, yes. Charisma preceding him by five miles in all directions, yes. But that mug?)

Anyway, as soon as Vincent Parry breaks out of San Quentin, he's in trouble. What has he done? He has chosen **A** over **B** and wound up with **C**. Now he has to avoid getting caught, which would not only endanger his life but also lengthen his prison sentence.

His choices are:

C: *stick around where he is*, or

D: *get the heck out of there*

So he starts getting the heck out of there. He gets an offer of a ride. Should he take it?

E: *take the ride and risk being identified*, or

F: *keep walking and make slower progress*

He decides yes. He's taking **E**. He hops in, and in short order it turns out this driver is quite a Nosy Parker and is about to identify him according to police reports now being broadcast over the car radio.

He must choose to:

E: *keep riding and take whatever comes of being identified*, or

G: *get the heck out of that ride*

He decides on **G**, to get the heck out of the ride, but when he asks the driver to pull over, the man makes it clear he knows Parry's the recent escapee and, what's more, will turn him in.

He can:

E: *keep riding*, or

H: *hurt the driver to get the heck out of that ride*

He hurts the driver. (As well as being a necessary education on the mistake he made back with **E** and **F**—ratcheting the tension on his *next* choice—this is also a fuse laid waiting to flare up again later when he can least afford it. One event playing more than one role in the story: that's layering.) Then he's back on the road, this time disguised in the driver's clothes. He gets *another* offer of a ride. Should he take it?

The most important thing about making mistakes is the opportunity we have to learn from them. Has Parry learned from the last mistake? Does he now know better than to take a ride? Yes, he does. But does he also now know the police are announcing his break-out on the radio and asking local drivers to report him if they see him on the road? Yes, indeed.

What's he going to choose?

I: *refuse the ride and take his chances on the road*, or

J: *accept this second ride*

He's in a *really* bad bind now. This is worse than just sitting around waiting to die in prison! Making an impossible choice is so agonizing to the human animal we often choose not to choose, even if that means staying put and suffering the torments of hell.

Then the second character throws a twist into it—she not only insists he get in, *she calls him by name*.

His option paralysis has been too great, and when she tips the scales for him, he accepts her decision. He dives in.

And here Goodis gives him a little break. She's nice! She tells him how to hide in the back of her car—very convenient, that tarp back there—and she smuggles him past the police guarding the entrance to San Francisco at the Golden Gate Bridge. She even takes him home with her, slips him into her building, and loans him her shower. She's like his *guardian angel*.

Using Character

So now he has another choice to make:

K: *Take her at face value*, or

L: *find out what's going on — who is this woman, why is she treating him this way?*

Remember that characters always have powerful motivation for the things they do. They can't just be nice to our protagonists because *we* want to be nice to them. Our characters are not us.

Parry chooses **L** and asks her, and lo-&-behold she's got a clipping of a letter to the editor in his own defense, written at the time of his trial. It's signed Irene Janney. She says she's Irene Janney. Irene likes Vincent, and apparently she *has* liked him for a long time without his knowledge. But *why*?

Again: every character in fiction has enormous, overpowering reasons for doing the things they do. *None of this is coincidence.*

So he has another choice to make:

M: *believe whatever she tells him*, or

N: *find out for himself*

He chooses **N**. After he showers, he searches her room, and — what do you know? — there's a whole scrapbook of clippings of the news reports of his arrest, trial, and imprisonment.

What's going *on* here?

And so it goes.

We have two essential points to learn from Goodis:

1) Everything our protagonist does causes the next effect. That's right — even in fueling momentum, it's always cause-&-effect. While Parry doesn't know it, he not only caused Janney to stop for him on the road, but he even caused her to be out on that road at the same time as him in the first place, conveniently beladen with a tarp under which a man could

hide. How did he cause that? *Oooh,* that's the Backstory! And it's coming up next. It turns out she has *extremely powerful reasons* for being interested in his welfare, reasons rooted, it so happens, in her very natural love for her own father.

2) The more difficult we make our protagonist's choices, the more complex the reasoning they must navigate in order to make the right choice, and the bigger the sword we hang over their head, the more intensely the reader is invested in reading all the way to the end to find out how our protagonist finally rids themself of this excruciating sequence of cause-&-effect.

As soon as Vincent Parry learns why Irene Janney is helping him, he realizes he has to find out who framed him, because that involves not only **protecting himself from the law** but also **protecting his guardian angel's father.** He's basically honorable, and he has a *need* to believe in the justice behind laws, even more now for this woman who's done so much for him.

Increase his need.

Also now that he's spent some time with this adoring babe, he and Janney have begun falling in love, so he no longer just wants **to live** he wants **to live for love**.

Again—*increase his need.*

But he can't find out who framed him so long as his face is on Wanted posters all over San Francisco. Unless, perhaps, he can choose to lose his face.

And the next thing we know, our protagonist is walking around San Francisco looking like Humphrey Bogart!

Using Character to Addict Your Reader

Now we know how to both discover plot and fuel momentum with character. Is that everything? Must we turn to

Using Character

other aspects of fiction for the addictive quality we know our story needs?

Not yet. Because character is not only the source of all plot and the fuel for all forward motion, it contains the most *fundamental addictive quality* that exists.

Readers read to learn how to survive. And our characters know how to do this. (If they don't, they'd sure better learn.) That's plot. Meanwhile, constantly increasing the momentum keeps the reader in a state of intense belief that the next page is going to teach them even more about survival than they've already learned. They can't wait!

But readers also read to learn life is *worth* surviving. And that reassurance is inherent in the very act of creating art—that deep, abiding, even paradoxical belief that the experience of living is worth preserving. It's worth the trouble of understanding. It's even worth the work of sharing. (And creating art others want to share is a *whole* lot of work.)

It was all worth it, after all.

We create this reassurance with rhythm, the push-pull rhythm at the core of all human experience.

There's a reason we crave that rhythm. It's the involuntary motion of breathing, the constant beat of pulse. It's the reverberation that made up our days and nights, our very instants, of the entire first nine months of life as we traveled hither and thither with our mothers listening to their hearts beat. That regular rhythm creates for us the moment-by-moment experience of being alive.

Mother in our senses! No, she's not there. Yes, she is! No, she's not. Yes! No. Yes! No. Yes! No. Yes! So passes all eternity.

Here's a protagonist with a need—something so true to their way of being they couldn't be themself without it. Maybe a woman needs freedom from fear of the occupying army that has taken over her rural village. She's a French woman, the conquerors are German, and aside from the long-standing animosity between the French and Germans for as long as either side can remember, the soldiers occupying her village don't just live here, *they own it*. They move into the houses, they patrol the streets, they monitor twenty-four hours a day the behavior and conversations of the locals whose land they have overrun.

Not only the woman but everyone she has ever known lives with the constant, inescapable adrenaline of fear. Fear of their lifelong enemy, the Germans. Fear for their lives. So whenever we show scenes of the woman under power of her need to survive—under power of this fear—we push the reader a little bit away. *Be afraid*, we say to them. *Be very afraid*.

At the same time, this woman is young and strong and healthy. She's married, so she's already an active sexual being. Her husband is gone—a prisoner of war, a philanderer with whom she was actually quite unhappy—and she lives with his mother, who doesn't particularly like her. The young German soldier billeted in their home is intelligent, kind, a musician. . .and *he likes her*.

Not only the woman, now, but everyone in the village is making allowances for the fact that these Germans, far from being simple monsters, are complex humans just as they are themselves. They have their strengths and weaknesses, their petty irritabilities and surprising moments of spontaneous generosity. So whenever we show scenes of the woman under power of her need to be liked, her need for intelligence, kindness, and music, her need for the tenderness that grows up between herself and the German soldier. . .we pull the reader deeply in. *There is love,* we are saying. *Even in the darkest night, love can still find us.*

Using Character

The struggle for survival. The reassurance that it's worth it.

Irene Nemirovsky's heart-breakingly beautiful novella *Dolce* uses her first-hand knowledge of life under the German occupation of WW II to inspire in us first the fear and then the love. It's hypnotic, the way she creates in the reader a *need* to be *reading this story*.

Over and over again, scene after scene. Fear, then love. Fear, then love. Fear. Love. *Fear. Love.*

Tension, then fulfillment.

Addiction. And resonance.

This is the paradoxical truth buried under everything we ever experience, in fiction and in life, from conception to death—this back-&-forth rhythm. It's the very rhythm of what it means to us to live.

Chapter 16

Layering Character
Believable fiction I

And so we come to the deepest, richest, most *compelling* aspect of character: **layering**.

Layering is bringing together all these approaches to character—developing, condensing, contrasting, motivation—to create levels within our protagonist that illuminate their internal conflict, those overwhelming conflicting needs that pit them against themself as they make their way through their adventures by the very skin of their teeth. All layering is based in the character's values, those things they *need*.

There is an infinite number of ways to layer character, just as there is an infinite number of characters to be created, with an infinite number of qualities on which to base their conflicting needs.

I'm going to talk about only three of the basics here, layering techniques so fundamental that they account for a ridiculously disproportionate amount of the fiction in the world today.

Layering Character with Behavior

Louisa May Alcott created layers to Jo March, but because she was writing about herself (and parts of herself she didn't fully understand) she didn't quite succeed the way she intended. We all believe Jo is gutsy, tough, smart, creative, and adventurous. Heck, yes. She put the "Oh, boy!" into tomboy. It's much harder to believe, though, that Jo is sincere in her protestations of devotion to the altruistic hogwash Alcott pasted over her character.

And yet, we *do* believe in Jo. We believe she's real. Why? What gives Jo her layering?

Her *tenderness*.

Sometimes Jo is running around the neighborhood wreaking havoc with Laurie, and sometimes she's sassing Marmee, and sometimes she's swashbuckling through the house pretending to take off pirate heads in the most dastardly unladylike way.

However, when Beth is dying Jo drops everything to be by her side—reading to her, caring for her, holding her hand and watching her slip away with tears in her eyes (tears Jo feels compelled to hide behind gruffness).

The ways in which Jo acts are always true to herself, true to her own values. And this means when the chips are down and her beloved sister needs her, Jo is there.

That's the layering that makes Jo a three-dimensional character and allows her to step off the page into the lives of her readers: her behavior.

We humans really *do* vacillate between our tough outer shells and the things that move our hearts. We do both flout authority and spontaneously give of ourselves. We do both make stupid mistakes and accidentally create flashes of light in another's darkness. The specific, detailed ways in which we do these things grow out of the specific values by which we live. Those details—the ways in which we act out our values— are the stuff of fiction.

Everything Jo does has its roots in the fundamental, conflicting values of her character. And because that makes her behavior real, she is believable.

Layering Character with Confusion

Eugene Henderson is an extraordinarily *ordinary* person. He's a bluff, hearty American businessman with a simple-minded socialite of a wife. He goes on business trips. In fact, he goes on a business trip to Africa. He knows he's ordinary. What are you going to do? It's just who he is.

So when Saul Bellow sent him, in *Henderson the Rain King*, on a bizarre pilgrimage to the heart of the African foothills in search of an elusive, little-known tribe, he had to give him good reasons. Bellow wanted Henderson blind to himself because he knew that confusion often leads to epiphany, and Bellow had specific things he wanted to explore within this particular epiphany.

So he gave Henderson a surface motivation to venture into that African wilderness. But at the same time, he gave him *hidden* motivation, reasons for going on this pilgrimage and sticking with it that an ordinary man like Henderson wouldn't normally have. And because those hidden reasons are rooted firmly in the values of Henderson the ordinary man, the fact that Henderson is oblivious to them doesn't keep them from being perfectly plausible motivation.

Eventually, the confusion Henderson has about his own hidden side leads him not only to the obscure tribe but to the tribe's inexplicable ritual for calling rain, a ritual in which Henderson—precisely because of his size and the very qualities of bluffness and innocent heartiness that make a man an ordinary American businessman—becomes inevitably entangled.

And the next thing Henderson knows, he's facing himself within the context of an experience that would be strange as hell even for the most *conscientiously* bizarre among us. Henderson has accidentally and through no fault of his own become the tribe's new Rain King.

Henderson's transformation from ordinary businessman to African Rain King is so implausible it would be simply impossible if it weren't for Bellows' meticulous, matter-of-fact record of significant details that allows the reader to experience the transformation with exactly the same level of oblivion and insight as Henderson. So by the time Bellows is done with us, we *are* Henderson the Rain King, trapped in an indecipherable reality from which we have no escape.

That innocent confusion is intensely real to the experience of being a human animal. And that makes Henderson—however unbelievable his story might be on the face of it—intensely believable.

Layering Character with Two Classical Needs

Vincent Parry is a canonical protagonist, caught between his need to live and his need to love. And I can't begin to tell you how much fiction—great literature, pulp, and everything in between—has been created through this straight-forward, eternal layering of these two most classical needs: **survival** and **love**.

Parry is simply an archetype.

David Goodis sent him into his story of *Dark Passage*, as so many protagonists are sent, running for his life from very real danger on page one. Violence! Injustice! Death! Oh, *no*! We all believe enthusiastically in a character's need to survive.

At the same time, almost the first person he meets is a *babe*. Flirtation! Sex! Passion! We also believe with all our hearts in a character's need to love.

So Parry's two conflicting needs are not unique to him at all. They're common to every human animal.

In fact, they're common to mammals in general. Everyone needs to live. And while we know only a little about how mammals aside from ourselves feel about each other, we do have evidence of powerful affection in their little mammalian hearts, and we honestly can't miss the proof of their overwhelming desire to copulate.

Back and forth, throughout the story, Goodis tosses Parry between these two most classical needs: survival, love—survival, love.

Every time Parry thinks he's on top of survival, something crops up in his need for love: his best friend dies mysteriously shortly after Parry visits him, then his nemesis surfaces, a woman he once rejected.

And every time Parry thinks he's on top of the love question, his life is threatened again: the Nosy Parker turns up, someone begins stalking Parry and Janney.

Until eventually Parry must choose between his safety and his passion for Janney—a nightmare choice, and the only possible Climax for his story, forcing him as it does to choose between his two overwhelming needs.

You recognize this, don't you? Of course you do. Nemirovsky used exactly the same needs—survival, love—for her gorgeous story, *Dolce,* although otherwise the two stories couldn't be more different.

James M. Cain used them for *The Postman Always Rings Twice.*

Emily Bronte twisted the daylights out of them for *Wuthering Heights.*

A protagonist trapped between their need for survival and their need for love: one of those few plots we have. Brought to life through all the myriad significant details of existence and humanity: *an infinity of stories.*

Plot is *Context*

Chapter 17

Designing an Impossible Plot with Maria Dermout

Once upon a time

There was a time when we could structure a novel like Maria Dermout's *The Ten Thousand Things* and get away with it.

I picked up *The Ten Thousand Things* in my local thrift shop because it was a 1950s hardback with nothing but the author's initials embossed in the center of the cover, and someday *I* intend to write a fifties hardback with nothing but *my* initials embossed in the center of the cover. There's something about them—the elegance. The restraint. The sheer courtesy to the author. "This is, after all, your book."

Then I started reading it and thought, *That's why I've never heard of Dermout. Because she didn't know how to plot.*

The first half of the book is a lush, multifaceted, fascinating portrait of an obscure garden estate—a 'spice park'—on some island somewhere in the ocean (at a rather random point near page 100 we learn we're in Java) in the early twentieth century. It seems longer ago because the story dates back six generations from there and even in the present the styles are quite old-fashioned—the characters wear batik sarongs with

Designing an Impossible Plot with Maria Dermout

little jackets over them, the women carry burdens on their heads, the little girls playing in the garden wear pinafores.

The only thing that looks even remotely like a plot is the fact that the little girls playing in the garden happen to be *dead*.

So we read along, and we're waiting for the dead little girls to do something interesting. But they don't. In fact, everyone eventually admits they've never actually seen them, just had them pointed out by others who claim *they* have. The girls were poisoned long ago, it seems. People think.

A child grows up in her grandmother's house on the obscure garden estate, goes to Europe with her parents, comes back as an adult with her baby son, and raises her son in her grandmother's house. The dead little girls remain just that—dead.

Around the middle of the book the grown son goes on an expedition to a local island as an officer and is killed by head-hunters.

End of that story.

Then we're in the second half of the book, which is a series of short stories: one story about the other ghost on the island, a man who has drowned on a beach near his creepy house, rumored to have been killed by his young wife and her three ancient aunts whom he kept locked in the house behind a high thorn fence; one story about the cook of the woman on the obscure garden estate, rumored to have stabbed an ex-lover to death until she is, herself, stabbed to death with his knife; and one story about a foolish European professor of botany who wanders willy-nilly through the islands, giving out polished coins to children in exchange for orchids and other rare flowers, until killed by four young men with machetes for his father's gold watch and his polished coins.

I'm thinking, *She just fell in love with this imaginary world of the islands and couldn't stop writing stories about it.* Because, to her credit, it really is a rich, vibrant, detailed imaginary world. And each individual story has a good, solid plot.

But this is not really a novel.

Finally, in the last story we're back with the woman on the obscure garden estate, and it is the night of the anniversary of her son's murder by the head-hunters, and the servants have gone to town, as they do every year, leaving her alone to mourn. Only instead of mourning, she's sitting in a rattan chair on the beach waiting for her annual visitors to arrive: the man who drowned, the cook and her ex-lover, the professor of botany, and—usually, but not always—her son.

The three little girls are there, too. They like the professor of botany. He's nice.

The woman has an argument with her son about death. She's adamant that the murdered are wholly different from those who die by other means, and she's quite annoyed the man who drowned doesn't know whether he was pushed or fell and doesn't seem to care.

Her son says, no, that's right, it doesn't really matter.

He says it isn't easy to die, whether you're killed or not, and his mother is furious with him for pretending. She says the murdered just don't want to admit the truth.

And this makes him laugh, which he has never done for her before.

Shortly after that they're all gone, and she is still sitting quietly in her rattan chair on the beach, and she whispers, frightened, for them to stay with her, but she's not sure now whether they were ever even there at all.

While she sits in the dark staring out at the moon path across the bay she sees coming toward her a *proa*—a boat—

Designing an Impossible Plot with Maria Dermout

carrying the mystical symbols of her life: a purple Palm of the Sea, a plate from Ceram, snails she calls the Sentinels of Good Fortune, a Crab for controlling the tide, and the nest of a holy Bird in the top of the Palm. There's a long list of magical talismans, and everyone she has ever known and loved is there. And all the murderers are there, because they belong there, too.

She wonders if she's dying, if these are her 'hundred things' that supposedly appear at the moment of death. But there are more than a hundred, there are a hundred hundred, and she can see no link between them except the spectacle of all of them together on this extraordinary *proa* coming toward her under the moonlight.

And then for just a split second...she sees the link. One moment of utter, focused brilliance flashing at the reader out of the depths of this gorgeous, seemingly-unfocused narrative.

And that's the Climax. The whole point of this story.

Later the woman's cook comes to fetch her, a simple Resolution of two paragraphs. She will go on living.

Sigh.

I want to tell you there was a time when we could write beautiful, ephemeral novels like this, when the reader didn't need to be dragged along by the hair but was willing to walk quite companionably by our side of their own free will. Because in those days we were reading for pleasure as much as escape, we had fewer things clamoring incessantly for our attention (less marketing by a thousand miles), we had — for lack of a better term — more peace of mind.

So when we're wondering about plots and sales and agents calling for fresh ideas and how to come up with some story that's never been told before, we must remember...

There was a time.

Chapter 18

Beating Your Drum

Introduction to holographic structure

It's incredibly difficult to get proper structure from the sheer feel of creating a work, and yet it's how so many of us approach writing.

Do you know the longest it can possibly take to write a novel by feel rather than plan? Neither do I. But I can tell you I once spent fourteen years on a novel without ever figuring it out. I finally sat myself down and analyzed *other people's* plots—great novels and stories—and read a book on screenwriting: *Screenplay* by Syd Field. So now I know how to do it. That part took about two months.

And I'm going to teach it to you.

Here's what we want out of plot structure:

We want to spark our reader's interest. Make them look up. Make them do a double-take in our direction. Make them say, *"What the heck?"*

Then we want to build on our reader's interest by showing them lots of interesting things happening to our protagonist. But we can't just pile a bunch of stuff together randomly, with no sense of order or chronology and without letting the reader know which things are more important than others and which things are *the most important things* of all. Because that just takes them to a flat plateau, and when we're standing on one, a flat plateau is indistinguishable from a flat plain. Boring.

So we organize the most important events we want to show our reader in increasing order of tension, from least to most. And for every one of those events:

We want to spark our reader's interest in that *one* event. Make them jerk their head around. "Who did *what*?"

We want to build on our reader's interest by showing them a variety of interesting things related to this *one* event. But we can't just create a smaller plateau. So we organize all the interesting parts of this *one* event in increasing order of tension, from least to most. And for each *one* part of this *one* event:

We want to spark our reader's interest in that part. Make them snap their mouth open. "Did it *how*?"

We want to build on our reader's interest by showing them new and complex and intriguing bits about this *one* part of the *one* event. We organize these bits in increasing order of tension, from least to most. And we show them to the reader.

We give our reader a second to integrate it all. That's our beat.

Then we reward our reader for their interest in this *one* part of the *one* event by showing them *the coolest bit there is to this one part.*

Then we go on to the *next* part of the *one* event and repeat that whole step, a spark followed by organized bits with a beat and reward.

We keep doing this until we run out of interesting parts to this *one* event.

We give our reader a minute to integrate the *last* part of this *one* event. That's our beat.

Then we reward our reader for their interest in this entire *one* event by showing them *the most exciting part there is to the one event.*

Then we go on to the *next* event we're going to throw at our protagonist. And do the whole thing over again.

We keep doing this until we run out of events for this story.

We give our reader some time to integrate the last event. That's our big beat with a backbeat.

Then we reward our reader for their interest in every single event in this entire story, all the anguish and chaos and recovery we've forced on our protagonist. We show the reader *the most important event of all.* Total meltdown! This event is the reason we're telling this story.

And if we're really, really nice, we throw in a Resolution on the final page for good measure, one last beat.

The End.

You can see, when we do this, that we wind up with a pattern, in which the very first part is gripping:

HOOK
"What the *heck*?"
"Who did *what*?"
"Did it *how*?"
And it settles into a rhythm:
"And *how*?"
"And *how*?"
Beat.
"Oh! *That's* how!"

CONFLICT #1
Which blows up in their faces:

"Whoa! They did *what* then?"
"Did it *how*?"
And it goes back to the rhythm:
"And *how*?"
"And *how*?"
Beat.
First Plot Point, end of Act I: "Oh! *That's* how!"

CONFLICT #2
And it blows up even worse, in what now turns to be a major rhythm:
"Whoa! They did *what* then?"
"Did it *how*?"
And there's the minor rhythm again:
"And *how*?"
"And *how*?"
Beat.
Fulcrum, midpoint of Act II: "Oh! *That's* how!"

CONFLICT #3
And it blows up again, a real crisis:
"Whoa! They did *what* then?"
"Did it *how*?"
And there's the minor rhythm again:
"And *how*?"
"And *how*?"
Beat.
And this time the big beat's got a little backbeat:
Backbeat.
Because this time the major rhythm kicks someone's butt:
Second Plot Point, end of Act II: "*Ow! That's* how!"

FAUX RESOLUTION

And this time the beat is a major beat:

Beat.

Beat.

Beat.

Startle your reader for a second with a little poke:

"*Wowza!*"

Go back to the beat:

Biggest backbeat of all.

CLIMAX

And now it's going to blow up irrevocably, once and for all, and our reader can feel the tingling in their bones:

"Whoa! They did *what* then?"

"Did it *how*?"

And there's the minor rhythm for the last time, quicker and more powerful than ever:

"And *how*?"

"And *how*?"

Beat.

And finally the reader unexpectedly learns the answer to the question they asked way, way back in the very beginning, "*What the heck?*" Which answer makes all their hair stand on end.

It's the whole point of our story, the end of Act III: "*Aghghghgh!* That's *what the heck!*"

Then we either provide the very, very final beat in the last moments of Act III or leave the reader flying through the air forced to provide that beat for themself.

Keep them baffled, clinging to the chandelier. And *coming back for more.*

Chapter 19

Designing a Crescendo
Explication of holographic structure

We talked about Hook, Development, and Climax in *The Art & Craft of Fiction: A Practitioner's Manual*, so we should all be familiar with these terms. A computer professor once told me studies show it takes fourteen iterations to work an idea into the human brain, so assuming you've read and re-read *The Art & Craft of Fiction*—which I am *certain* you have—poring over it through the long, winter's night, hunched by candlelight in your garret under the cold, rainy eaves...we'll call this iteration #7.

As playwrights and screenwriters have known for eons, all stories are constructed chronologically from a basic set of building blocks. Because fiction is so dense and novels are so long, I break them down into their six parts: Hook, Conflict #1, Conflict #2, Conflict #3, Faux Resolution, and Climax.

But these can also be understood under a larger umbrella known as *three-act structure:*

Act I: Hook
Act II: Development
Act III: Climax

I lump them together roughly this way:

Act I: Hook
HOOK
CONFLICT #1

Act II: Development
CONFLICT #2
CONFLICT #3

Act III: Climax
FAUX RESOLUTION
CLIMAX

The thing to remember about the three acts of three-act structure is that each episode is constructed, internally, exactly the same way the story is constructed as a whole, that is— hook, development, and climax. And *that* means:

Act I: Hook

HOOK
- Hook
- Conflict (1-3)
- Faux Resolution
- Climax

CONFLICT#1
- Hook
- Conflict (1-3)
- Faux Resolution
- Climax

Act II: Development

CONFLICT #2
- Hook
- Conflict (1-3)
- Faux Resolution
- Climax

CONFLICT #3
- Hook
- Conflict (1-3)
- Faux Resolution
- Climax

Act III: Climax

FAUX RESOLUTION
- Hook
- Conflict (1-3)
- Anti-Faux Resolution
- Climax

CLIMAX
- Hook
- Conflict (1-3)
- Faux Resolution
- Climax

I know it looks like formula. But it's not. This is primal rhythm, the one we just bongo'd out in the last chapter.

Yank! Boom, boom, boom. A beat. *Boom!*

Designing a Crescendo

Sit with it for a minute. Mess around with it a little—two or four booms, multiple or no beats, multiple or no yanks, multiple final *booms!* or none at all. Push the rhythm to the limit of as much build-up as humanly possible without going too far. Balance the elements against each other. Notice what feels most like riding a falling avalanche on a toboggan.

Feel it in your bones.

Now, take a good, hard gander at that list. Notice that if we include the full three conflicts in each episode (we don't have to, but we shouldn't do more than three, or our build-up will become long-winded), we wind up with—thirty-six pieces. Which is a rather convenient divisor of the 72,000 words that are these days commonly considered minimum for a novel. Particularly if we make a point of averaging either 1,000 or 2,000 words per scene, depending upon our own internal rhythms.

Do the math. Take your time. Because this piece of information is absolutely *incredible*.

It means it's perfectly possible to plan an entire novel *scene-by-scene*. Either thirty-six scenes of approximately 2,000 words apiece. Or thirty-six episodes each containing two scenes of approximately 1,000 words apiece. Or some combination of the two.

Not only *that*—it means when all those scenes are written the whole thing not only hangs together with unshakable cohesion, but it builds in tension, modulates pacing with breath-taking accuracy, and reaches the best and brightest, most spectacular catastrophe at exactly the right instant to blow the reader right out of their chair.

Haven't you ever wondered how pulp writers of the Golden Age of vintage fiction did it?

This is how.

Aspiring pantsers have *no idea*. Yes, Stephen King and Flannery O'Connor could feel their way through this blindfolded. Raymond Chandler and Agatha Christie did it, too. But nobody has to. And it's far, far easier to take off the blindfold and just watch where we step.

Chandler wrote only seven novels in his entire lifetime. His close friend Erle Stanley Gardner cranked out so many books he had to use half-a-dozen pseudonyms to deal with them all, and the Perry Mason mysteries alone number over seventy.

Structure.

Vintage pulp's gift to us.

Fatal Ignition

What the authors of vintage pulp knew that literary artists were assumed not to know is that readers read for thrills. They want to see the characters dynamited, they want to see it big, and they want to see it *now*.

Although there was a period in literary history in which great artists like Dermout could assemble their fuses, explosives, and igniting sparks at their leisure, these days the necessity for a quick *bang!* is taken as a given by almost everyone in the publishing industry. That's what agents look for in manuscripts, it's what publishers' acquisitions editors look for, it's what the marketers and bookseller reps who sit in on publishers' acquisitions meetings look for.

Thrills.

Occasionally we'll hear someone who doesn't understand the industry very well bewailing this situation. "All you slummers want is sensationalist low-brow genre!" Or the other side of the coin, "All you stuffed shirts want is dry, high-brow literary gobbledygook!"

But thrill is what readers of all types of fiction have *always* wanted, as Edward Anderson showed us at the beginning of his beautiful Dustbowl novel *Thieves Like Us, a romance,* when Bowie, his insides twisting, watches a car come bumping slowly down the old dirt road toward him where he waits in his convict's clothing under the shadow of a prison wall.

Anyone who's ever watched a movie that begins with a release from prison (and they are legion) knows they don't release you in your convict's clothing. And so we understand this is a story about an escaped con—about *thieves*, we are told, *like us*.

And this does indeed turn out at the Climax to be exactly what this story is about.

The Hook scene, although not the most important moment in our novel, is the most important moment in the *career* of our novel.

Especially in today's publishing climate, when tens of thousands of newly-hatched aspiring writers are being urged and exhorted every day to query agents and publishers' acquisitions editors with the first-draft fruits of their uncoordinated infant efforts at fiction, nobody in the industry has more than a few seconds to glance at any particular manuscript and decide then-&-there whether or not they want to see the rest.

"Am I intrigued? Am I *thrilled?*"

First scene. Character, plot, and prose must all combine in a primeval quark of almost unimaginable mass right there on the first page. We must ignite that fuse, make it short, dynamite our reader out of their chair.

We'll have time later to pick up all the pieces and assemble the puzzle.

Backstory

What is it? Why is it important? And what on earth are we supposed to *do* with that stuff?

As little as humanly possible.

It's true that Backstory plays a part in proper plot structure. Sometimes we need a little illumination from behind the curtain. A little light filtering through the lace, highlighting the pattern as it begins to move. However, extra information is awkward, it requires its own special techniques, and the reader prefers to get that information the way they get almost everything else these days — on the fly.

So before we start throwing on the flood lamps and ripping holes in the fabric of our story, we must spend a good long time spelling out all that information in great detail in our notes and identifying ways to layer it into our characters' interactions and adventures.

The reason Backstory is so often confused with exposition is that they share a lot in common:

- lack of momentum
- lack of in-the-moment excitement
- lack of mystery

You see? All lacks. *Not* a good quality in storytelling technique.

Everything we put into a story must add to the forward momentum of our plot. It must be about getting our characters from point (x_1, y_1, z_1) to point (x_n, y_n, z_n) with as much velocity as humanly possible. We are here to make our characters' lives a hellbent-for-leather ride. When we stop the action in order to explain what's gone before or what's going on now — to point at

Designing a Crescendo

the curtains—we throw our reader right into the dashboard. They don't like that. They like their hair flying straight back off their heads.

Our job with Backstory is to make sure it does not throw our reader into the dashboard.

At the same time, everything we put into a story must serve the purposes of pacing. Most of what readers want out of pacing is increasing tension to make previous excitement look like the slow part laying the groundwork for what's *really* electrifying.

Now, there are subtle undulations that we, the writers, know we've layered into this increasing tension. But the reader is feeling the pulsing increase in pressure of G's that—if all goes well—is going to eventually implode on them, blasting them into a parallel universe. When we stop adding significant description, action, and dialog to keep that pressure stimulating, soothing, stimulating in carefully-modulated doses—when we lift the G's to pause and discourse on general stuff—it feels weak. And our reader is likely to lurch out of our grip and fall like a lump back to earth while they're still under the sway of gravity.

Our job with Backstory is to make sure it keeps our reader forever entirely engaged in the thrilling experience of the story, heading into orbit.

Finally, our story must always be about launching our reader out of our imagination and into their own, the curiosity that impels them out into the ether. When we drag the story backward with Backstory or exposition, we're dragging the reader's attention back to ourselves. And they don't want to pay attention to us. Then want to pay attention to themself, to their own experience of this mysterious, rocketing ride through the wilds of the imagination.

Our job with Backstory is to make sure our reader is *always* wholly engaged in exploring our fictional landscape, completely forgetting there's a human being behind it all typing frantically away.

Ray Bradbury helped bring dark literary (pre-'edgy' 'edgy') fantasy and sci-fi to the forefront of modern fiction through his meticulous, unerring instinct for pure scene without a speck of exposition. And in "The Dwarf," the first story in his literary masterpiece collection *The October Country*, Bradbury teaches us *exactly* how to handle Backstory.

Instead of telling us in exposition what the Dwarf has done before the hook scene of his story's Hook, Bradbury shows the owner of the carnival Mirror Maze telling the protagonist, innocent Aimee, how the Dwarf has come to him more than once in the past asking about the price of his funhouse mirrors.

Bradbury places this Backstory exactly right, directly between the Hook and Conflict #1, and he ties it back into the Hook by introducing the conversation through Aimee's observation that the Dwarf almost came up to them after he'd been inside the Mirror Maze, almost asked something he just couldn't bring himself to ask.

This gives the owner of the Mirror Maze the opportunity to tell the story of the other times the Dwarf has come to him and almost asked where he could buy such a mirror, something he couldn't quite, in the end, bring himself to ask.

That's Backstory with forward momentum, ominous tingling, and ever deeper curiosity about Bradbury's special melancholy country of inner torment.

And it's only what's *absolutely* necessary.

We must winnow our Backstory down to only that most essential information the reader simply *has* to have as they venture into our story, layering as much of that as possible into

Designing a Crescendo

the process of our characters getting to know each other, and casting what's left (if anything) into either very brief exposition or — better — thoroughly vivid flashback scenes.

We put those flashback scenes into Chapter Two or Three, after the Hook, before we get too deep into Conflict #1.

But only what's *absolutely* necessary.

Three Acts

And now we've launched our reader into the first of our three acts: Hook, Development, Climax.

So let's talk about the purposes of these three acts, since they serve as the building blocks of pretty much *all* storytelling, in one form or another. Yes — they're that powerful.

Act I is the set-up: we're setting our protagonist up like a bowling pin. What the reader really wants out of a good story is to see the protagonist knocked down so hard they bring the bowling alley down on their heads. That doesn't happen in Act I, though. Act I is the set-up. Set your protagonist up *really well*.

Act II is the big game: the reason we don't leap straight from Act I to Act III is that stories are *fun*. Especially really long stories like novels. They're rich, complicated, devilishly entertaining. A good story chases the reader around the corral with the lasso swinging — *thwip thwip thwip* — over its head until it's thrown it and got them by one hind leg, and then it drags them in circles through the dust and mud and cow-pies while they shriek with glee. Does the lasso matter to how the story ends?

It's *essential*.

Finally, Act III is the pay-off: the catastrophe our reader has come here to witness. There's some fancy footwork we do, some classic shuffling we employ to make that final *whallop* as vast and deep and supremely satisfying as humanly possible.

But this is where the bowling alley collapses. Breaks the water main. Bursts the gas lines. And the next thing you know, our reader is staggering out of a cloud of smoke like 1906 San Francisco, coughing and squinting, with singed hair and a staggered gait, their hands groping blindly in front of them.

Utterly *thrilled.*

In 1934 James M. Cain blew the lid off genre thriller with his classic novella *The Postman Always Rings Twice,* not-quite 120 pages. It's written with such gorgeous, dark *noir* detail that no one's ever cared there's no postman in it and, in fact, no one to ring the doorbell twice. . .or even once.

In perfect three-act structure.

Act I

On the first page, the protagonist, Frank Chambers, turns up at the roadside diner at which he will eventually rob, kidnap, and finally kill. In fact, in the first sentence he gets thrown off a hay truck right in front of it. Now, *that's* a Hook!

Cain needed Frank to commit the pivotal crime around which he intended to structure his story, so that's Act I—setting Frank up.

Frank meets the Greek who owns the diner and, in short order, meets the Greek's wife, Cora, for whom he develops an instantaneous hot flash that takes over his entire awareness and rides him from that moment to the very end. It turns out Cora's got the same hot flash for Frank, and between them they're in the sack quicker than you can say cat-on-a-ladder.

Frank doesn't want to kill the Greek. Frank's not the killing kind. Neither, really, is Cora. But she's trapped in that marriage, as so many young women of her era were trapped.

Even more, that diner is all she's ever earned through her own hard labor and common sense, and it's in the Greek's name. She needs to get out, to be with Frank. And she also needs to keep the one valuable thing she owns (conflicting *needs!*).

At the same time, Frank, who needs not to get entangled in nefarious illegal stuff, realizes he also needs Cora (conflicting *needs!*). And he finds himself in the throes of sexual passion agreeing to help her.

So Frank and Cora go through with their plan to kill the Greek, which involves conking him unconscious in the tub. However, while she's upstairs in the act, Frank and a passing cop watch a cat climb the stepladder Cora's supposed to use to escape, and as soon as the cop pulls out of the driveway there's a flash and all the power goes out. Cora botches the job in the dark, and she and Frank wind up having to save the Greek so the botched attempt won't be obvious. It turns out at just the wrong instant the cat stepped off the ladder onto the fuse box and electrocuted itself.

These guys are *born losers*.

Now they need a *second* plan. Which is twice as hard to plan and carry out, now that they've got that close call on their consciences. (And on the reader's.) But this one works! Against all odds—truthfully, both Frank and Cora are kind of surprised. The Greek is dead, and their lives have suddenly altered forever.

Page forty, $1/3$ of the way in. End of Act I.

Act II

Because Frank and Cora were present when the Greek died, they're investigated, and Cora winds up on trial. Frank's involved. There's a DA who forces Frank to point the finger at Cora in order to be cleared of suspicion himself. Then Frank's lawyer arranges for Cora to confess the truth to a private detective she believes is a cop, so she won't blurt it out in court. It's all quite complex, but again, weirdly enough, it works. They planned it carefully, and even when their plans backfire the lawyer saves them in the eleventh hour through fancy machinations with the insurance companies who have insured the life of the Greek. Forty of the most hair-raising pages in the literary canon, and suddenly Frank and Cora are going home to the roadside diner, not only free of suspicion but with ten thousand dollars of the Greek's insurance money in their pockets.

Page eighty, $2/3$ of the way in. End of Act II.

Act III

And after drama and mayhem and terror...this is where things get *bad*.

Because the lawyer's detective goes renegade, he has Cora's confession, and he's a blackmailer. But even more than that, Frank has gone a little renegade himself, done a little philandering behind Cora's back, and now the whole business about Frank having sold Cora out comes back to haunt them.

This is cause-&-effect. This is plot grown straight out of character. And it's handled simply brilliantly.

The purpose of three-act structure is to set the protagonist up, knock them down, set them up, knock them down, and then set them up *really big* while the reader's heart is still trying to get out their throat. It's the quintessential Third Time's a Charm.

By the end of his novel, Cain has Frank and Cora exactly where he wants them, in the core of their very worst nightmare, on the bullseye he aimed them toward way, way back in the beginning, when he gave Frank that shove off the

Designing a Crescendo

hay truck in the very first sentence on page one. And he has the reader clinging to the chandelier.

If you were an unskilled blue-collar drifter type during the Depression Era,

And you got away with murder to the tune of $10,000,

But you put yourself in a position to lose trust in the one person you absolutely needed to trust in order to stay clear of the electric chair...

What would you do?

Exactly what Frank and Cora do at the Climax of *The Postman Always Rings Twice*.

Two Plot Points

'Spin.' Those two structural supports at the ends of Acts I and II that fling our characters willy-nilly off one trajectory and onto another.

These are the climaxes of Conflict #1 and Conflict #3. (There's also a climax to Conflict #2, of course, which we'll get to later.)

We saw how James M. Cain spun his characters with a vengeance when he constructed the three acts of his canonical spine-tingler. First he gave them what they wanted. Then he gave it to them *again*. Wow — we'd better all be careful what we wish for!

But can it be done with a more sedate story, a longer plot structure, a less deadly premise?

Zane Grey's classic Western, *Riders of the Purple Sage*, tells two intertwined stories:

1) That of the young cowpoke Venters, nearly flogged to death in Chapter One by the Mormon Elder of a little Utah town, Tull, for being too close to the woman who owns the

town, the unmarried and independent Jane Withersteen. In his constant struggle to keep from being killed by either Tull or the bandits known to hide out in the local canyons, Venters shoots a masked rider who turns out to be a young woman held captive by the local bandit king, Oldring, and whom Venters must hide in the wild and beautiful Utah canyons until he can nurse her back to health.

2) That of the Gentile outlaw Lassiter. Too smart for Tull, too tough for Oldring, only Lassiter can save Withersteen from Tull's heartless efforts to acquire her as one of his Mormon wives and the ownership of the entire town along with her.

So what spins their stories?

First of all, 280 pages of novel means the $1/4$-point arrives on page 70 and the $1/3$-point around page 93, the $2/3$-point around page 187 and the $3/4$-point on page 210. These are the approximate ends of Acts I and II.

This is important. We don't know yet whether Grey likes to put the end of Act I closer to $1/4$ or $1/3$ or the end of Act II closer to $2/3$ or $3/4$. (We saw that Cain slammed them down right on the $1/3$ and $2/3$ marks.)

However, with this heavily layered a story, Grey's given himself some room to maneuver. How does he do it?

Act I end, first Plot Point, pages 70–93

On page 70, Lassiter is stumbling at the end of a chapter up a long slope toward Withersteen, having just saved an entire herd of her cattle that's been maliciously stampeded by Tull's men in order to terrify Withersteen, cost her thousands of costly head of cattle, and humble her into submission—the first dreadful showdown between Tull and Withersteen.

That was the **first climax of Act I**.

Withersteen owns the fastest and most beautiful horses in the region, and when Lassiter arrives at her feet and pants out that his horse is dead, she offers him not only one of her prize horses but also the position of main rider on her ranch. Although up until now she's hoped she could call a truce between Tull, the leader of the Mormon Church in which she fervently believes, and Lassiter, the maverick Gentile she trusts, Tull has just forced her down off the fence between them and drawn the battle line.

This is the **first resolution of Act I**, which 'spins' their story in a new direction.

And so sides are chosen.

Meanwhile, Venters, feeling simply terrible about having nearly killed the innocent Masked Rider, is carrying her in his arms deeper and deeper into the canyons where the bandits she's escaped can't find them. He's discovered a wonderful valley high in the hills beyond nearly impassible crags, and this is where he carries the wounded young woman, at great physical cost to himself. On page 89, he's actually climbing his lasso up a sheer cliff face with the woman's limp body in his arms.

That's the **second climax of Act I**.

And on page 91, the end of a chapter, they have arrived at a cave at the mouth of the valley, where he informs her under the night sky that she's finally safe from the bandits she so fiercely hates.

This is the **second resolution of Act I**, and it 'spins' *their* story in a new direction.

The new chapter on page 92 begins with Venters' exploration of the magical valley where he's going to spend the bulk of the book. And so his current goal—saving the life of the young woman he's shot—becomes another goal—making a home for them both here in the wilderness.

End of Conflict #1 and Act I.

Spin!

Act II end, second Plot Point, pages 187–210

Now, Venters has been busy for the past 94 pages since we left Act I. He's been up and down the canyons, back to Withersteen's ranch and up to the valley again, working secretly to feed and support the young woman even while hiding her existence from everyone, even his employer. He's gotten to know Lassiter pretty well, but he hasn't even told *him*.

And on page 187 the young woman, still recovering, gives an almighty scream that brings Venters running like a madman, in terror that Oldring has discovered them at last.

This is the **first climax of Act II**.

When he arrives he finds—what do you know?—Lassiter standing bemusedly over their campfire. He doesn't mean them any harm. He's just finally followed Venters back up the torturous canyon paths to find out what the heck is going on out in them thar hills.

This is the **first resolution of Act II**, and again it 'spins' the story of Venters and the woman in a new direction.

From here on out, Venters is no longer a man with a secret. He is a man *revealing* his secret and struggling to resolve it safely within the context of his greater world.

This sets him up for the big showdown at the novel's Climax with Oldring himself.

Meanwhile, just like the chapter about the stampeded cattle at the first climax of Act I, the chapter at the second climax of Act II is an all-out hellbent-for-leather race across the chaparral. Tull's right-hand man Jerry Card has killed one of Withersteen's hired hands and stolen her prize horses—including one belonging to Venters called Wrangle, who's always been a bit unpredictable although he's fast as the dickens. Venters is hot on Card's heels, knowing if he succeeds at stealing the horses Tull has won the battle against Lassiter and Withersteen.

This chapter has the reader hanging onto their hat with both hands from the first page. And it's only at the very end of the chapter that Venters finally catches up with Card, after Card has ridden to the brink of death and abandoned Withersteen's number one prize horse and transferred in mid-flight to the hot-tempered but fresher Wrangle.

This is the **second climax of Act II**. And it's a *humdinger*.

On page 208, Venters has reached the cliff edge upon which Wrangle is—bizarrely—dancing madly with Card clinging to his neck. Venters realizes this is what's been odd about Wrangle all along: he's simply not right in the head. And now he's lost it completely. The horse has gone mad.

At the end of page 208, Venters is wasting bullets trying to shoot the horse before Card gets control of him and escapes.

Venters fires his last shot. The horse, still carrying Card, cartwheels off the cliff.

On page 209, in the final short paragraph, Venters hears the rumble of the avalanche the falling horse has triggered.

Boy, *howdy*.

Second resolution of Act II.

Truly, there's no way around it now. Lassiter and Withersteen are heading into the novel's Climax, facing Tull down in person, loaded for bear.

End of Conflict #3 and Act II.

Super-duper spin!

Now pay close attention: the law of cause-&-effect means every one of those spins was *earned* by the preceding actions of the characters.

Earned.

Of course, we don't need both first *and* second *anything* at the ends of our Acts. Grey did that because his two nearly-parallel plotlines (remember that all novels have two nearly-parallel plotlines) are so far apart they don't actually merge until the novel's Climax. And that means they give good examples of different ways to design those 'spins.'

In most novels, the climaxes and resolutions that spin the stories are just single events in which the two plotlines crash into each other and bounce off again. (Frank and Cora kill the Greek. Frank and Cora are almost taken down by the investigation.)

But you see how Grey with his distinctly separate plotlines kept them detailed and varied all the way through, so when they each reach the ends of his Acts he could spin his characters' stories, once and then once again, to keep the reader guessing every step of the way where it's all headed.

And in this manner, he managed to give hundreds of thousands of readers throughout the ages *the ride of their lives*.

One Fulcrum

Although we get those all-important two Plot Points from three-act structure, there's yet a third leg to this extraordinary storytelling stool: the *mid-point*.

I call it the Fulcrum. Where everything pivots from light to dark.

Designing a Crescendo

Halfway to ²/₃ of the way through our novel—just about halfway through Act II, as a matter of fact—something simple and yet earthshaking happens to our characters: they stop moving away from their Hook and begin moving toward their Climax.

In a mystery, this is when the second poor sap dies.

While the first Plot Point (the climax of Act I) is the climax of Conflict #1, and the second Plot Point (the climax of Act II) is the climax of Conflict #3, this Fulcrum is the climax of Conflict #2, right in the middle.

At this point, we have laid all our fuses. We've introduced the protagonist and any other characters essential to the Climax. We've created and arranged the separate tracks convening upon inevitable catastrophe, the whole reason we're telling this story. We've given our protagonist the two loggerhead needs that are driving them relentlessly toward that catastrophe, and we've ratcheted the pressure on those needs, exaggerating and enhancing them until our reader can't distinguish anymore between the protagonist and themself. Now we need to give the hourglass a good, solid shake. Settle the sand before we flip the whole thing over and let time begin to run out...

In 1764, Horace Walpole launched not one but several of today's healthiest genres with his wonderful black comedy, *The Castle of Otranto*. Although at not-quite 100 pages too short for the delicate sensibilities of most of today's agents and publishers, *Otranto* is the original gothic novel (gothic 'romance,' in the terms of Walpole's day, meaning a story for entertainment rather than a moral lecture), the root of both gothic fiction of the nineteenth century and today's popular horror/thriller/paranormal genres. Although in the nineteenth century Mrs. Radcliffe took the ball and ran with it right through the goalposts—wow, did she—it was Walpole's rascally little handbook on how to tweak the noses of the literati that first kicked the whole thing off.

And, sure enough, right there on page 50 of *Otranto*, something enormous happens. The one character standing in the way of the villain's agenda *dies*. Sadly, he's been squished by a ghost's giant helmet.

Up until that moment, the villain Manfred, Prince of Otranto, has been struggling to free himself of both his lawful and rather dizzyingly submissive wife Hippolita and his son Conrad, the betrothed of young Isabella for whom Manfred has suddenly developed a terrible case of the racing hots. Someone (not Manfred) has dropped a giant marble helmet on Conrad—bummer about that. There goes Manfred's competition. Unfortunately, Isabella has recently had the unmitigated gall to not only repulse Manfred's advances but take shelter under the protection of her father's knights.

What's a Prince got to do to get a *little service* around here?

But now, just halfway through the novel, Manfred has an unexpected stroke of luck. His son dies of the terrible squishing. Poor Conrad! His pride and joy! Child and heir! Bootjack over which he's tripped incessantly since he first got a load of young Isabella in her nightie!

And this heartens Manfred so much he is struck again, this time by divine inspiration. He rushes to give the news of Conrad's death to Isabella's father's knights, along with the information—*oh, heartbreak!*—that as much as he loves his dear wife to whom he would fain cleave in conjugal bliss...they've discovered they're too-close kin. Their marriage cannot produce a legal heir.

Given these two circumstances, Manfred explains in all heartfelt guilelessness, it really would be best for everyone

Designing a Crescendo

involved if Isabella were surrendered up to him for immediate conjugation.

Now, we won't examine too carefully the claim that in Walpole's day it was quite possible to *accidentally* marry too-close kin. Even as recently as the early 1900s, my own great-grandparents were free to marry their second cousins (which they promptly did), and a generation before that my great-great-grandparents were free to marry their *first* cousins (each other). Even granting enormous families—and my German ancestors produced nothing if not enormous families—it seems a bit far-fetched to think that in 1764 you could marry someone even closer than that and not even notice.

Who would that have to be? Your *brother*?

But let's take very good note of when this amazing switch in Manfred's fortunes occurs: exactly halfway through his story.

Because up until this point Isabella, Conrad, Hippolita, and the mysterious stranger lurking in the castle's subterranean catacombs, as well as the friar of the local monastery and Bianca the faithful maid (*nobody* wants Manfred to wind up with Isabella), have all had a chance. Isabella was betrothed to Conrad. Sure, he wasn't exactly her idea of a hot night in Rio. But he was okay. He'd do. At least he wasn't a lecher, like his father.

And after the Fulcrum everything's changed. Manfred's not going to have any trouble shucking Hippolita, we already know, because as much as she wrings her hands and dribbles tears down the front of her embroidered shift, she's too much of a doormat to put up a fight.

Now it's up to Isabella and her defenders, of whom the most powerful—her father—isn't even present. The friar can shield her to some extent. Bianca is willing to stand up for her.

But, truly, Isabella's best bet lies in casting herself upon the mercy of the mysterious stranger, the charming young buck of the catacombs for whom she's already feeling more than a peck of pheromonal interest: that swashbuckling tasty treat, Theo.

(I know—Theo's actually in love with Conrad's sister and the friend of Isabella's bosom, Matilda, but she conveniently dies in time for Isabella to get her man in the end. It's just too bad he feels compelled to live out his life of conjugal bliss sunk in melancholy over the loss of the toothsome Mattie. Walpole had a *very dark* sense of humor.)

And we can see how this change of fortunes throws the burden of the story firmly onto the shoulders of the protagonists—far more so than ever before—as they cease to run higgledy-piggledy in all directions, searching for an escape route, and begin to thunder with concerted deafening tread in the direction of their—supposed—saving grace.

Feinting

So let's talk a little about that fascinating element directly *before* the Climax of a novel: the Faux Resolution.

I named it.

Yay me.

But I didn't invent it. No, the Faux Resolution has been around forever, generally thought of (if it's thought of at all) as the denouement to Conflict #3, the beginning of Act III right before the Climax.

It's something more than that, though. Something much, much more.

Isak Dinesen was an absolute fiend with plot. She didn't study plot structure, but she did have a fabulous innate sense of it. (Geniuses get to have such things.) Of course, since she *didn't* study it her plots wouldn't really stand up to today's rigorous genre-dominated standards—they're almost jazz riffs. But her innate sense led her true.

Dinesen knew pacing like the back of her hand, and she used it to keep her reader hooked throughout endless permutations that morph almost compulsively from one chronological layer to another, as her characters discourse on religion, society, history, gender roles, even the ultimate definition of truth.

She built and built and built her stories in tension, as they morphed through their multiple layers, until she had the characters hanging from a cliff by their fingernails.

Then she did something diabolical.

She threw them a rope.

Unfortunately, she didn't *tie* it to anything. So when her characters let go of the cliff to reach for it...

In the first and most canonical of her *Seven Gothic Tales*, "The Deluge at Norderney," Dinesen takes the reader through the life stories of four unusual, complex souls trapped together overnight during a rising flood, fully aware that they are all on the brink of death, only to finally marry off one young couple (strangers to each other) and force the others (an elderly Cardinal and even more elderly, virtuous madwoman) to confess to each other their darkest secrets.

Just before the Climax, after the married young couple has fallen asleep holding hands and after the dreadful, profound confessions, the elderly madwoman insists the elderly Cardinal kiss her so that she will not die unkissed. Although he's just confessed to assault and impersonation, he realizes she's right—their confessions have, in a strange way, been as much a wedding ceremony as the one they've so recently performed for the young couple.

So he kisses her. Her life is vindicated.

That's why it's such a shock when she lifts her hem in the next sentence, the beginning of the Climax, and hands it to him to show him their high, dry loft has begun filling with water. The flood has caught up with them.

When we talk about plotting a novel, we must by definition talk about pacing. I like to think of this as the Great Fictional Rollercoaster, which we induce our reader to ride by luring them into the cars with the bright, shiny carrot of our novel's Hook.

"Come along, little one," we say. "Step right in. Settle down. Fasten your seat belt. Why a seat belt? *Nice* shiny carrot. See the pretty carrot? Keep your eyes on the shiny, dangly carrot. All comfy? That's right...*take 'em, Joe*—"

And they're off.

Down, down, down we drop them into the depths of the Hook, gasping and clutching the rail with wide, popping eyes. Up, up, up they go to the lead-in to Conflict #1, where first they take in the view ("Wow! Cool view!") and then leave their lunch behind when they go plummeting straight down into the bowels of Conflict #1, flying off the end of Act I shrieking at the top of their lungs.

Up, up, up we bring them, climbing into Conflict #2. "Hey! There's that great view again! It's even *better* from here—" Down, down, down they plummet, shrieking even louder to the depths of Conflict #2. Up, up, up into Conflict #3, so high they're standing up on the seat when we drop them like a rock back down again at the end of Act II.

Up and down, up and down, all the way through our novel. And all along we're also bouncing them like yo-yos holographically, in telescoping replicas of the overall Rollercoaster. *Ka-boing. Ka-boing, Ka-boing. Ka-boing.*

Designing a Crescendo

They're a puppet in our hands. The Master.

Until we've finally dropped them off the end of Act II so long and so fast and so hard that they've left not only their lunch, but their teeth, eyeballs, and most of their internal organs back at that last view and are now not much more than a trembling skeleton, a shadow of their former self, a complete minion to our every whim.

Power. You bet. That's why people write.

And now we take a little pity. Not too much. Nobody wants too much pity. But just the tiniest smidgen, a gentle, kindly hand smoothing their fevered brow.

"Mommy," our reader whimpers. "Big freaky plotline go *boom bang boom!*"

This is the Faux Resolution. It's the point at which we finally give our reader a break. Have we shaken them to the core? Made their hair stand trembling on end? Yanked them right out of their shoes?

We rock them in our arms. Stroke their hair. Give them a little smooch. "I was only kidding," we tell them. "I don't really hate you. All in the service of the story, you know."

And they buy it. "We know. We weren't really scared. Just a little. Startled, really. You caught us off-guard, that's all. We're fine now."

"Of course you are." Rock, rock. Stroke, stroke. Smooch, smooch. "All better? Aren't you glad you went for that ride? Wasn't it the most exciting thing ever?"

"*Unbelievable,*" they're saying. "We are so coming back again, the instant we are fully recovered —"

"Did you really love it?"

"We loved it. We *loved* it. You are the Fiction Goddess."

We sigh. "I'm so glad you feel that way..."

Yank goes the cord. *Bam* goes Joe.

"*Aaaaaghghgh!*" goes our reader, as we shoot them point-blank, top speed at the Climax, which they hit with such force it smacks an epiphany out of the deepest reaches of their raw subconscious soul.

The Whole Point

What's the Climax of a novel?

We must understand, for now, only this one, fundamental thing: the Climax is the *real reason we write our stories*.

Once upon a time, two teenagers became so distraught over their passion for each other they committed suicide—that's the premise. Cause? Their parents wouldn't let them marry or even date—that's the story. Cause of that? Their families hated each other—that's the backstory.

—*Romeo & Juliet*, William Shakespeare

Once upon a time, a man succumbed to idiocy over the death of the woman he loved—that's the premise. Cause? His rival for her love stole her from him and then killed her in anguish over the betrayal he'd committed against a saintly man—that's the story. Cause of that? His rival was an old and close friend of his—that's the backstory.

—*The Idiot*, Fyodor Dostoevsky

Once upon a time, a woman nearly lost the man she loved through her own machinations—that's the premise. Cause? She was an inveterate social meddler—that's the story. Cause of that? Although good-hearted, she had always been spoiled—that's the backstory.

—*Emma*, Jane Austen

Designing a Crescendo

Once upon a time, a woman became so distraught over her adulterous affair that she committed suicide—that's the premise. Cause? Society ostracized her for her affair, while at the same time her lover made her intensely jealous—that's the story. Cause of that? She was a married female aristocrat of nineteenth-century Russia with an intensely passionate nature—that's the backstory.

—*Anna Karenina*, Leo Tolstoy

Once upon a time, a man encountered a ghoul and disappeared—that's the premise. Cause? He was out at night after spending the evening competing with another man for the love of a young woman—that's the story. Cause of that? He was an unattractive schoolteacher in a highly superstitious time and place, with a ruthless and contemptuous rival—that's the backstory.

—"The Legend of Sleepy Hollow," Washington Irving

Do you see how the Climax is, bizarrely enough, the *premise*? We must dwell on this in the depths of our soul until it makes total and complete sense. Mull it over. Meditate upon it. Make it a part of our writing identity. We cannot take this fact too seriously.

The Climax is the whole point.

Otherwise, we have no reason for writing any of this.

Chapter 20

Hook

Holographic structure, Act I

We're going to do something long and slow and meticulous, now.

We're going to walk step-by-step through the six stories I've used to demonstrate the different parts of structure: Edward Anderson's historical novel, *Thieves Like Us, a romance*; Ray Bradbury's brooding 'edgy' story, "The Dwarf"; James M. Cain's *noir* thriller, *The Postman Always Rings Twice*; Zane Grey's Western adventure, *Riders of the Purple Sage*; Horace Walpole's black comedy, the gothic/horror/thriller/paranormal romance, *The Castle of Otranto*; and Isak Dinesen's mystical literary fable, "The Deluge at Norderney."

These are classics of their genres, the roots from which all such stories today have sprung (although some modern genres appear on the surface to be quite different from their roots, as is the case with Western adventure and post-apocalyptic adventure).

We're going to uncover, piece-by-piece, all the parts in all the stories to learn—once and for all, down to our bones—how *all* great stories, of *all* genres, use the same building blocks to create the imaginary worlds in which we love to dwell.

Act I: Hook

The first thing a reader reads when they open a novel or short story is the Hook—that first most exciting episode that occurs to start these characters down the path trying to resolve the conflict between their two intense needs.

And the first part of *that* is the hook of the Hook (because of course each of the six basic elements has its own basic elements—lending the entire discussion its quintessential Dr. Seuss air).

And the first bit of *that* is the *hook scene*. (The hook of the Hook is often just that one scene. But not always.)

And the very first words—those few precious, optimally-powerfully words that pull the reader in and make them want to read the next words—that's the *hook sentence*.

Hook

Hook sentence

In *Thieves Like Us*, Anderson shows us a car trundling with difficulty down a rutted road off the highway toward someone waiting.

In "The Dwarf," Bradbury shows us his protagonist, Aimee, quietly and with implied expectation gazing around.

In *The Postman Always Rings Twice*, Cain shows us his protagonist, Frank, being hucked off a hay truck in front of a diner.

In *Riders of the Purple Sage*, Grey shows us a messenger leaving one of his three protagonists, Jane Withersteen. (A *rider*. Across the *purple sage*.)

In *The Castle of Otranto*, Walpole shows us wealthy Prince Manfred and his children, Conrad and Matilda. (This expository type of introduction wasn't common even in Walpole's day, but it certainly was for the era in which he was *pretending* to write, the twelfth century.)

And in "The Deluge at Norderney," Dinesen shows us a Danish seaside resort of the early 1800s at a time, she says, when the people of Northern Europe still regarded the ocean as their age-old 'demonic' enemy.

Hook scene

In *Thieves*, the protagonist Bowie waits with his friend Chicamaw under the prison wall in their convicts' clothing for the car to reach them, and Bowie asks Chicamaw if he's really committed to their plan.

In "Dwarf," Aimee meets up with her friend Ralph, the owner of the Mirror Maze, and he tells her carnivals are the easiest places to die if that's what you want, bringing up as an example a dwarf regular of his.

In *Postman*, Frank wanders into the diner and begins to pull his standard con on the Greek who owns it.

In *Riders*, Withersteen reflects upon the message she's just received, which demands she hand over her Gentile hired help, Venters, to the local Mormon leader, Tull. Withersteen, who is a faithful Mormon woman, tries to shield Venters when Tull arrives, even as Tull prepares to whip Venters for being too friendly with Withersteen, until a stranger on horseback unexpectedly interrupts—the infamous maverick Gentile outlaw, Lassiter.

In *Otranto*, Manfred's subjects raise their eyebrows over his plans to marry off his sickly son Conrad to his daughter Matilda's best friend, the delectable Isabella, gossiping that his haste is based on a prophecy of doom to his sovereignty over the Castle of Otranto.

Hook

And in "Norderney," fashionable ladies and gentlemen brave proximity to the sea for the sake of rubbing elbows with dukes, princes, and merchant aristocracy, even as the local peasants remember the monstrous hidden danger.

Spend some time studying these six beginnings. Notice what goes into the *hook sentence* and what can wait to be illuminated in the full *hook scene*. Pay particular attention to the clues to fundamental, inherent conflict in the hook scenes: the convicts' dependence upon each other, death at a carnival, a drifter's con, violence based upon religious conflict, a prophecy of doom, and high society under the shadow of mortality.

These are all clues to these stories' Climaxes. Right there — *on the first page.*

Development

So, after they're initially hooked, the reader reads the Hook development, how that first hook scene builds upon itself (always aiming toward the whole point of the Hook). This occurs in a series of one to three conflicts, which may be longer or shorter, depending upon the length of the story and intentions of the writer.

In *Thieves*, Bowie hops out of the car in which their third partner, T-Dub, has picked up Bowie and Chicamaw. Bowie waits by the side of the road while Chicamaw and T-Dub head off to look for the friend who's going to hide them out, and when they don't return for Bowie he watches for them all night in the rain.

In "Dwarf," Ralph shows Aimee, who doesn't really want to know, how to spy on the Dwarf in the Mirror Maze.

In *Postman*, Frank establishes rapport with the Greek and meets his wife Cora, to whom Frank is instantly intensely attracted, although he admits she's more disturbingly unhappy than lovely.

In *Riders*, the backstory of the Hook is cast in a scene in which Lassiter tells Withersteen he's come to town to find the grave of a Milly Erne, who, it turns out, was once Withersteen's closest friend who died of a broken heart years ago when the Mormons kidnapped her little girl because she refused to raise her Mormon. Lassiter and Venters make friends, both of them loyal to Withersteen.

In *Otranto*, Manfred's plans for the wedding of Isabella and Conrad are interrupted when the servants rush in in hysterics to inform everyone that Conrad has been squashed underneath a giant marble helmet and is now dying. The helmet turns up missing from the enormous marble statue of the original owner of the Castle of Otranto, Alfonso, from whom Manfred's ancestor inherited it when Alfonso died during the Crusades.

And in "Norderney," a dreadful storm create enormous sea pressure, which, after the end of the storm, breaks the dikes and floods the lowland where the resort lies. The four main characters are the last of those being rescued by boat when they come across a barn loft containing a woman and her children.

Again, mull all this over. Take notes. Examine how the Hook is being built upon, bringing in complications, forcing the characters to cope, *immediately* and *without mercy*. The writer puts their characters in the soup and makes them struggle—when they're struggling, that's when they show what they're made of, and *what they're made of* is exactly what the reader's reading for.

You see how this is all heats up within the *first five pages*? (Although we're not going to reach the climax of the Hook until either $1/8$ or $1/6$ of the way into the entire story, leaving room yet for plenty of Hook development between page five and that climax.)

And now we know how agents and publishers can make decisions on whether or not we've got a good, gripping story so early in the manuscript.

Act I: Hook climax—*Fatal Ignition*

Now we're reaching the whole point of this Hook, which I like to consider the story's *Fatal Ignition*.

The reader has become intrigued by the build-up of this Hook and deeply curious about where it's all going.

Well, *we* know where it's going! It's going toward the whole point of the Hook, that first most exciting episode, the Fatal Ignition that sets these characters struggling valiantly against themselves.

But first...

Faux Resolution

That build-up takes an unexpected detour at the last minute and culminates in the faux resolution of the Hook. *Yippee!* Disaster averted!

In *Thieves*, morning brings dry weather, Bowie feels better, and he gets a ride on a passing wagon into town.

In "Dwarf," the Dwarf goes straight to a room that makes him look tall and dances beatifically in front of the mirror.

In *Postman*, Frank establishes himself over the ensuing weeks as the Greek's right-hand help around the diner, even while he also shares a brief, passionate grope with Cora.

In *Riders*, Withersteen takes Lassiter and Venters to see Milly's grave, where they all bond.

In *Otranto*, Isabella, fighting off the advances of Manfred, descends to the castle dungeons, where she stumbles upon a gracious and very good-looking young scamp willing to help her escape.

And in "Norderney," a Cardinal and an elderly madwoman volunteer to trade places with the woman and her children trapped by the flood in the loft, followed quickly by the madwoman's fierce young companion and an unknown young man, all of them anxious to be a part of this rescue operation. They each have their reasons for this—all character behavior is based upon authentic motivation—although the reader doesn't know yet what they are.

This faux resolution creates a beat in the storytelling rhythm, a significant pause to bring out the full resonance of the climax. Fiction is about contrast, so watch carefully how the contrast between the faux resolution and the climax of the Hook creates a visceral vibration *inside the reader*.

Climax

Finally the reader reaches the whole point of the Hook, which is that first exciting catastrophe that starts the story's entire avalanche—whatever event the writer has designed to illuminate for the characters (for the very first time) exactly what they're up against—the climax of the Hook.

In *Thieves*, Bowie arrives in town and has to guess that a stranger he meets is the man in charge of their hide-out, taking a gamble on revealing himself without knowing for sure, even as the young woman he's going to fall in love with watches—suddenly he's risking his very neck just when he thinks he's finally escaped.

Hook

In "The Dwarf," as the Dwarf dances with joy at his reflection, Ralph sniggers contemptuously at him—suddenly Aimee realizes her friend is hostile to the Dwarf.

In *Postman*, Frank's passion for Cora leads him, in a moment of sexual light-headedness, to agree to help her kill the Greek—suddenly he's committed himself to this crime for the sake of passion.

In *Riders*, Withersteen realizes Lassiter might be Milly's long-lost husband come to avenge her death against Tull and the Mormon Bishop Dyer—suddenly Withersteen is trapped between loyalty to the man who's come here for the sake of her dead best friend (and who saved Venters when she couldn't) and loyalty to her religion.

In *Otranto*, Isabella just barely escapes as Manfred appears, accidentally leaving the adorable stranger to Manfred's vicious clutches—suddenly the three of them are caught up together in the story's deadly *ménage a trois*.

And in "Norderney," the Cardinal and elderly madwoman admit to the others they have almost no chance of surviving the night, as the flood waters are deep and moving and the building beneath them will probably collapse out from underneath them before sunrise—suddenly they all face the fact that they're going to die.

So you see how the writer has lead the reader skillfully from a single *hook sentence*, through illumination of that sentence in a *hook scene*, into tension and conflict built upon that hook scene, with a subtle little dodge at the last minute to make the impact of the climax truly unexpected...and then sprung the hidden purpose of the Hook on the reader without warning while they're looking the other way?

Wow, there's a leap in the gut for the reader! Reader involvement—reader *investment*.

Now we're approximately $1/8$-$1/6$ of the way into this, and the reader's full, undivided, viscerally-stimulated attention is Hooked.

So the writer can begin to tell their story.

Act I: Backstory

But first the writer slips in whatever Backstory they need. Remember: only what's *absolutely* necessary. And, if at all possible, layered into the characters getting to know each other.

In *Thieves*, the owner of the hide-out, Dee Mowbley, fills them in on the law enforcement in the local town and explains just enough about his daughter Keechie for the reader to understand she's a pivotal character.

In "Dwarf," Ralph tells Aimee a brief story about the Dwarf wanting very badly to buy one of the mirrors that make him look tall.

In *Postman*, there's no full Backstory, just a leap straight into the hook to Conflict #1.

In *Riders*, there's no full Backstory, as it's all been told already in that scene in the backstory of the Hook.

In *Otranto*, yet again, there's no full Backstory.

And in "Norderney," the narrator gives the Backstory of the elderly madwoman in exposition. (Dinesen's narrative voice is intensely old-fashioned, so although she wrote lovely scenes she also knew how to write marvelous exposition—as was common two hundred years ago, the era in which most of her stories are set.)

Act I: Conflict #1

Whew! Hooked by the gills! Thrown up in the air and just about to be caught deftly again in the writer's brilliant web.

Once again, we're at a hook, this time the hook of Conflict #1, which is going to culminate eventually in the whole point of Conflict #1, its climax: the story's *first Plot Point*.

And the first bit of *that* hook is the *hook scene*.

And the very first words — those few essential words that pull the reader in and make them want to read the next words — that's the *hook sentence*.

Hook

Hook sentence

In *Thieves*, T-Dub says Keechie gave him the evil eye when she first saw him.

In "Dwarf," Aimee addresses Ralph urgently to get his attention — she has something important to ask.

In *Postman*, what appears to be a trivial piece of dialog is illuminated a few lines later as a staged scene meant to lead into murder.

In *Riders*, one of Withersteen's riders appears, his horse in a lather.

In *Otranto*, Manfred hears the trap door close after the escaping Isabella.

And in "Norderney," the Cardinal begins to tell his life story describing how, as a boy, he knew a famous Danish painter who claimed a washed face is the only truthful face.

Hook scene

In *Thieves*, After Dee assures Bowie, Chicamaw, and T-Dub that Keechie will take care of them while he's working, the others talk over their new life—how to avoid the Laws when you travel, who's most likely to snitch on you (a sore woman), and, most important for justifying their lives as armed bank robbers, how politicians prove they're "thieves," too, "just like us."

In "Dwarf," Aimee asks Ralph why he doesn't sell one of his old mirrors to the Dwarf.

In *Postman*, Frank goes downstairs as look-out while Cora approaches the Greek in his bath to murder him, and a cop stops by to see what Frank's doing. The cop has just left when the lights blow out.

In *Riders*, Withersteen's rider tells her one of her herds of cattle has been stampeded by rustlers.

In *Otranto*, Manfred, incensed, squares off against the young stranger, Theodore, who misleads him so he won't catch Isabella.

And in "Norderney," the madwoman laughs at the Cardinal's idea that God wants the truth from humans.

Again, be aware of what goes into the *hook sentence* and what waits to be illuminated in the full *hook scene*. You'll see now how the clues to conflict in these hook scenes of Conflict #1 relate to the climaxes of Conflict #1 (not necessarily the stories' Climaxes, but one step removed): the convicts' relationship to the Laws and political collusion with lawbreaking, the *ménage a trois* of Aimee, Ralph, and the Dwarf, the murder of the Greek, the stampede of Withersteen's cattle, Manfred's pursuit of Isabella, and the difficulty of meeting a moral goal in this material world.

The climax of Conflict #1 is going to crystallize the extremes of the characters' dilemmas, the poles between which they ricochet—creating another visceral vibration in the reader.

Hook

Development

Now, after they're hooked on Conflict #1, the reader reads the Conflict development, how that hook scene builds upon itself, revealing new aspects of the story never seen before while elaborating upon elements first introduced in the Hook (and always aiming toward the whole point of Conflict #1). Just as in the Hook, this occurs in Conflict #1 in a series of one to three conflicts, which may be longer or shorter, depending upon the length of the story and intentions of the writer.

In *Thieves*, Keechie turns up, and she and Bowie start falling for each other. Bowie, Chicamaw, and T-Dub read about their prison break in the newspaper and make plans to move on. Bowie learns more about Keechie's life and confides in her that he plans to quit bank robbery and go straight. However, first he and the others head for a new hide-out, planning one last job.

In "Dwarf," Ralph admits he could get a second-hand mirror for thirty-five dollars but refuses to help the Dwarf buy one, explaining to Aimee the Dwarf wouldn't take it, and even if he would he couldn't afford it, because, after all, where can a Dwarf earn money outside circus freak shows?

In *Postman*, Frank rushes upstairs, and Cora tells him she fumbled it in the dark, only stunning the Greek and not killing him. They call an ambulance, and the Greek goes to the hospital and is saved.

In *Riders*, Venters rides out to save Withersteen's cattle herd, and in a shoot-out with the head rustler, Oldring, shoots Oldring's legendary Masked Rider. Venters is appalled to learn, when he stops to help him, that the legendary Masked Rider is actually a young woman trying to escape the rustlers.

In *Otranto,* Manfred's servants, again hysterical, inform him they've come across a giant lying full-length in the castle gallery and blocking the door with his foot.

And in "Norderney," the young man tells the story of how he was raised the son of a skipper and then favored as a teen by a rich Baron who turned out to be his real father, so that in his despair over losing the father he loves for a rich man who has deceived him, he has run away.

Now the characters are struggling harder and harder all the time. And as their struggles become more protracted, they're forced to reach deeper into their souls for the resources with which to cope. And that's when they show what they're made of, because, as we remember, *what they're made of* is what the reader's reading to find out.

Act I: Conflict #1 climax— *First Plot Point*

So we're reaching the whole point of Conflict #1, which is the story's *first Plot Point*.

The reader has been drawn in by the build-up of this Conflict and is anxious to learn where it's all going.

Of course, *we* know where it's going. It's going toward the whole point of Conflict #1, that first Plot Point, which is going to turn the characters on their heads and completely bamboozle them, sending them off in a new direction they simply do *not* expect.

But first...

Faux Resolution

That build-up takes a quick detour at the last minute and results in the faux resolution of Conflict #1. *Thank goodness!* Things are looking up!

Hook

In *Thieves*, Bowie and Chicamaw settle down for a few days in their new hide-out and tell stories, laughing over Chicamaw having been thanked once by a cop for not killing him when he could.

In "Dwarf," Aimee says facetiously she's in love with the Dwarf, trying to lighten the tone of the conversation while pushing Ralph away a little.

In *Postman*, on their way home from the hospital, Frank guides Cora through dismantling the 'slungshot' they made out of ball bearings in a sack, so no one will ever know what they almost did.

In *Riders*, Venters carries the young woman he shot high into the canyons until he discovers a hidden valley with an entrance guarded by an enormous Balancing Rock, where they can hide from Oldring.

In *Otranto*, Hippolita is the only one who can soothe Manfred.

And in "Norderney," in the young man's story, his father, the skipper, finds him and comforts him with the information that he has gold buried in Haiti the young man can have.

Again—there's that beat. The characters take a breath. The reader looks the other way...

Climax

And finally the reader reaches that whole point of Conflict #1, which is that first Plot Point—the first huge event that spins the characters' story and sends them whirling off in an unexpected direction, still madly fleeing their Hook—the climax of Conflict #1.

In *Thieves*, Chicamaw tells Bowie about the Laws shooting men they don't like in front of banks in order to collect huge rewards for dead bank robbers, "thieves" of the public coffers, "just like us," explains what it's like to live in the lap of luxury in Mexico, and finally describes a deadly Texas prison farm where inmates are deliberately worked to death and sometimes killed outright—suddenly they have both an exotic, hopeful goal and terrible, deadly danger to avoid.

In "Dwarf," Ralph, who is in love with Aimee, pretends to be amused by Aimee saying she's in love with the Dwarf, although he's not amused at all—suddenly he's intensely jealous, which makes him a secret threat to the Dwarf.

In *Postman*, the cop comes back, suspicious of Frank, and insists on looking at the fuse box. That's when they find the dead cat, and there's a brief, exhilarating resolution when the cop concludes the cat stepped off the ladder onto the fuse box and blew the fuse—suddenly Frank is both terrified of the cop's suspicions and impossibly relieved there's no proof to support them.

In *Riders*, in a hellbent-for-leather, rip-snorting chase scene across the sage, Lassiter saves Withersteen's cattle herd, which has been deliberately stampeded, and she asks him to be her rider, offering him one of her prize horses. Meanwhile, Venters carries the wounded young woman, Bess, through the steep entrance to the hidden valley—suddenly both pairs of characters are allied for the long-term against their two enemies, Tull and Oldring (who, the characters don't yet realize, are in cahoots).

In *Otranto*, Manfred, all but rubbing his hands in evil glee, plots to use Hippolita's blind loyalty to gain her cooperation in acquiring Isabella—suddenly his power to destroy Isabella's life takes on real credibility.

And in "Norderney," the young man refuses his father's gold, but accepts his advice to take to the sea—and suddenly

Hook

he is, like the others in the loft, loose in the dangerous world all on his own.

Again, spend some long, deep, thoughtful hours with all this. Take your time. Take your notes. Examine how the Hook has roped the characters in and Conflict #1 thrown them a live coal, so that Act I becomes a whole, blistering, brilliant flash of lightning upon a situation for which these characters are not prepared and to which they're only now being fully, painfully awakened.

They're threatened! They have a glimpse of hope! The poles of their dilemmas are crystallized!

Now we're approximately $1/4$-$1/3$ of the way into this story, and the reader's *invested*.

So the writer can turn up the heat.

Chapter 21

Development
Holographic structure, Act II

Act II: Conflict #2

Deep in drama! We're done with Act I and forging into Act II.

We've passed the first Plot Point, the characters' trajectories have shifted significantly, and the ends of the spectrum upon which they struggle are beginning to come into focus. Things are more intriguing than ever.

And, yet again, we're at a hook, this time the hook of Conflict #2, which is going to culminate eventually in the whole point of Conflict #2, its climax: the story's *Fulcrum*.

And the first bit of *that* hook is the *hook scene*.

And the very first words — those few gripping words that pull the reader in and make them need to read the next words — that's the *hook sentence*.

Development

Hook

Hook sentence

In *Thieves*, Bowie, Chicamaw, and T-Dub rent a furnished house where they can stay awhile.

In "Dwarf," we feel the warmth of a summer night turning through morning to the heat of afternoon. (Bradbury tosses in a wonderful descriptive sentence after that first one in this brief hook paragraph—he's a whiz with wonderful description.)

In *Postman*, all Frank can say is that they didn't do anything about *anything*. Their relief over escaping a bungled murder of the Greek is too overpowering.

In *Riders*, Venters is lying in the starlight and then gloom of dawn in the hidden valley.

In *Otranto*, Manfred's daughter Matilda is restless.

And in "Norderney," the madwoman offers to tell the story of her young companion, Calypso, describing the uncle who raised the young woman as a man obsessed with spiritual matters.

Hook scene

In *Thieves*, Bowie, Chicamaw, and T-Dub admit they are low on money, so they plan a bank robbery.

In "Dwarf," Aimee tells Ralph she's discovered the Dwarf is a brilliant, tormented writer. She reads the Dwarf's writing aloud to Ralph, amazed that he's so much smarter and more talented than either of them. She says she can't stand the unfairness of life, that she and Ralph can choose between the carnival and normal life, while the Dwarf's body limits him to being a carny.

In *Postman*, Frank and Cora, in bed together for the first time while the Greek is in the hospital, swear they will never try anything so insane as murder again.

In *Riders*, Venters tends to the young woman's wounds and learns how much she hates herself and the life she's led with Oldring, so that he promises himself he'll take revenge upon Oldring for her.

In *Otranto*, Matilda is telling her maid Bianca she's in love with the portrait of her ancestor Alfonso when Bianca hears a ghostly voice, which turns out to be Theodore, the captivating young man of the catacombs, singing out the window of his cell in the dungeon in which Manfred has had him flung. Matilda flirts with Theodore, and Bianca informs Matilda that Isabella is hiding out at the local monastery.

And in "Norderney," the madwoman tells how Calypso's old uncle taught her to hate being a woman, until she saw her own naked body in a mirror and very nearly took a hatchet to herself in loathing, only to be saved by the sight of happy, naked nymphs in an ancient tapestry.

Once again, be aware of what goes into the *hook sentence* and what will wait to be illuminated in the full *hook scene*. The clues to conflict in these hook scenes of Conflict #2 relate to the climaxes of Conflict #2 (not necessarily the stories' Climaxes, but one step removed, just as in the climax of Conflict #1): the convicts' return to bank robbery that will narrow their hopes for the future down to simple escape from the Laws, the way in which the Dwarf illuminates Aimee's growing separation from Ralph, the bond between Frank and Cora that will narrow their prospects down to pulling off a murder, the uniting against opposition of Withersteen and Lassiter, of Venters and Bess, the squaring off of Manfred against Isabella and Theodore and Matilda, and a passion for embracing life while we still have it.

Development

The climax of Conflict #2 is going to close the door on alternative futures and focus upon driving the characters relentlessly toward the story's Climax.

Development

Now, after they're hooked on Conflict #2, the reader reads the Conflict development, how that hook scene builds upon itself, revealing the last of the essential new aspects of the story, getting down to the real nitty-gritty here as we hone in on the Fulcrum that's going to flip this story on its back, tying everything together with elements already introduced in the Hook and Conflict #1 in Act I (and always aiming toward the whole point of Conflict #2). Just as in the Hook and Conflict #1, this occurs in a series of one to three conflicts, which may be longer or shorter, depending upon the length of the story and intentions of the writer.

In *Thieves*, Bowie, Chicamaw, and T-Dub pull first a small bank robbery and then a larger one and are in an accident during the second get-away, which brings the police. They get in a shoot-out with the police when they refuse to stick around to make a statement.

In "Dwarf," Aimee pulls thirty-five dollars out of her purse and tells Ralph she's going to buy the Dwarf that mirror he wants so badly. Ralph tries to dissuade her, but she's determined, until he slams out in anger.

In *Postman*, Frank and Cora have a happy week, then they begin fighting. They try to run away together, but Cora chickens out. Frank does run away, and when he comes back the Greek is home, thrilled to see him, and Cora is desperate to get rid of Frank before she falls in love with him again. She confesses to Frank that the Greek wants children now, and she's thought she could go through with it so long as she never saw Frank again.

In *Riders*, Lassiter settles down as Withersteen's right-hand man. Withersteen's friends among the Mormon women all urge her to marry Tull and get it over with, and only a dying Gentile woman, the mother of Withersteen's favorite little child, Faye, tells Withersteen she'll trust her to raise Faye so long as Withersteen promises not to raise her Mormon. Unexpectedly, Lassiter learns Withersteen has only been pretending to be fond of him in order to keep him from killing Tull and Dyer—she really doesn't know him well enough to feel true affection.

In *Otranto*, Manfred hot-foots it over to the monastery after Isabella, where he learns Theodore is the son of the friar, Jerome, and blackmails Jerome with Theodore's life.

And in "Norderney," the madwoman tells how, after her epiphany over her woman's body, Calypso went into her uncle's room with a hatchet while he was sleeping to take revenge upon him for teaching her his terrible misogyny, but instead she turned away at the last moment and escaped his house. The madwoman tells Calypso the young man now in the loft with them has sacrificed his life to be with her, and although the young man knows she is lying he is swept up in the thrill of her imagination and falls in love with Calypso.

Go ahead and once again study all this carefully. Make copious notes to yourself. Analyze how Act I is being built upon in Act II, complicated, illuminated, *developed*. The characters are handling a plethora of issues now that come at them from all sides—they're juggling, dancing, yodeling for all they're worth, constantly and with driving urgency. They're up to their necks in showing what they're made of. Because *what they're made of* is, of course, *what matters*.

Development

Act II: Conflict #2 climax— *Fulcrum*

So we're reaching the whole point of Conflict #2, which I've described as the story's *Fulcrum*.

The reader is halfway through the story now, completely beguiled by the build-up of this Conflict and desperate to find out where it's all going.

As you remember, *we* know where it's going. It's going toward the whole point of Conflict #2, the Fulcrum of the story, which is going to throw those characters from a black-&-white world into full-color.

But first...

Faux Resolution

That build-up takes a much-needed detour at the last minute and turns into the faux resolution of Conflict #2. *Holy smokes!* A last-minute reprieve!

In *Thieves*, Keechie shows up to nurse Bowie of his injuries from the shoot-out, and they reach an understanding.

In "Dwarf," Aimee calls the man who sells mirrors to Ralph, imagining the Dwarf waking in the cold in the middle of the night to dance beatifically in front of his tall mirror.

In *Postman*, Frank and Cora are on the road taking a holiday with the Greek, Frank and the Greek drunk and singing in the back seat and Cora driving.

In *Riders*, Withersteen and Lassiter come clean with each other—she admits she's been snowing him to protect Dyer and Tull from him, and he admits he meant to kill whoever was responsible for the death of Milly, and they have their first passionate love scene.

In *Otranto*, the knights of Isabella's father, Frederic, arrive to verify that her marriage to Conrad is going through as planned.

And in "Norderney," the Cardinal, at the madwoman's behest, marries the young man and Calypso.

This is a little bit bigger of a beat than the last faux resolution. This is a lovely beat, the first moment in which the writer flashes a quick revelation of the intense hopes and dreams for which these characters struggle so hard. Love! Beauty! Bonding! Truth! This is the point at which the writer begins to promise the reader, "They're going to make it."

Climax

Finally the reader reaches the whole point of Conflict #2, which is that pivotal Fulcrum—the moment the scales shift and the characters stop fleeing their Hook and begin pursuing with every ounce of passion in their souls something they don't yet know is going to turn out to be their worst nightmare, the Climax. That Fulcrum is the climax of Conflict #2.

In *Thieves*, Chicamaw, drunk and broke, turns up saying he's lost all his bank robbery money gambling—gamblers are "thieves"—and admits to Bowie that he knows, although he's a loser, Bowie's the kind of guy who will go straight. The problem is there's a reward out for them now, and Chicamaw, worried, says they're terribly hot, in real danger of winding up at the deadly prison farm in Texas. He brings out their guns, and he and Bowie plan their escape to Mexico—suddenly they're no longer escaping jail and building their savings, they're plowing headfirst through danger toward their dreams of safety.

In "Dwarf," Aimee gets ahold of the man who sells mirrors and cries out to him, thinking of the Dwarf's anguish—

Development

suddenly she's no longer following Ralph's lead, she's forging ahead toward her own solution to circumstances.

In *Postman*, in a carefully-planned sequence, Frank waits until Cora has driven them to a cliff edge and then kills the Greek with a blow to the head with a wrench—suddenly they're no longer trying to escape the urge to eliminate the Greek, they've done it and must move forward with the consequences.

In *Riders*, Lassiter proves to Withersteen she couldn't escape Tull and Dyer now if she wanted to, as she's watched constantly by men hidden in the sage around her house and by the women who work for her. They share a moment of anguished soul-searching over their internal conflicts—suddenly Withersteen no longer believes she can be reconciled to Tull and Dyer, she's cut loose from her church and even her home, and she must cope with a future she can't possibly predict.

In *Otranto*, Manfred announces to Frederic's knights that Conrad has finally died and Hippolita has turned out to be too close a relation to bear him lawful children, so he's going to marry Isabella himself—suddenly the characters are no longer playing cat-&-mouse with Manfred, they're forced to face his determined machinations head-on.

And in "Norderney," the madwoman suggests to the Cardinal the definition of 'humbug' might be sinners in hell pretending they have not been living in hell from the day they were born—suddenly they're not talking about how they've made their deadly sacrifice during the flood to save their moral lives, they're talking about what happens to our souls after we die.

The doors onto alternative futures have slammed shut, and the characters know now what they need and what will happen to them if they don't get it.

We're approximately $1/2$-$2/3$ of the way into this story, and the reader is feeling the balance of it swing portentously inside them, carrying them right along with it.

So the writer can get crazy.

Act II: Conflict #3

We've passed the Fulcrum, and we're no longer laying fuses in all directions. We're beginning to blow things up.

And once again, we're at another hook, this time the hook of Conflict #3, which is going to culminate eventually in the whole point of Conflict #3, its climax: the story's second Plot Point.

And the first bit of *that* hook is the *hook scene*.

And the very first words—those few seductive words that pull the reader in and make them want to read the next words—that's the *hook sentence*.

Hook

Hook sentence

In *Thieves*, Bowie lies in bed worrying about everything that frightens him.

In "Dwarf," night arrives, and again Bradbury makes a transition, as he so often does, with a simple, classical declarative sentence marking the passage of time.

In *Postman*, again, all Frank can say is that he and Cora didn't say anything (their chronic inability to say what they

Development

need to say when they need to say it is key to their dreadful downhill slide).

In *Riders*, Venters wakes in the hidden valley.

In *Otranto*, Jerome arrives at the castle from the monastery.

And in "Norderney," the Cardinal compliments the elderly madwoman on her insight, making her blush.

Hook scene

In *Thieves*, Keechie returns to take care of Bowie, and when she soothes his fears they sleep together.

In "Dwarf," Aimee fights with Ralph over the Dwarf.

In *Postman*, Frank and Cora stage the 'accident' in which the Greek will appear to have died, including beating each other badly.

In *Riders*, Venters and Bess are falling in love, safe in their hidden valley, which he's named Surprise Valley. He tells her about his horse, Wrangle, the fastest horse on Withersteen's ranch, although just a trifle unpredictable.

In *Otranto*, before Manfred can shut Jerome up, he announces that Isabella has vanished from the monastery, so Frederic's knights are alerted to Isabella's objections to Manfred.

And in "Norderney," the Cardinal tells the madwoman there are worse things than eternal damnation.

Again, be aware of what goes into the *hook sentence* and what is illuminated in the full *hook scene*. You'll see now how the clues to conflict in these hook scenes of Conflict #3 relate to the climaxes of Conflict #3 (not necessarily the stories' Climaxes, but the final of this series of steps once-removed): the—eventually tragic—love between Bowie and Keechie, Aimee's revelation of Ralph's true self, the extraordinary murder plot that teaches Frank and Cora to trust *no one*, the brilliant but unstable horse Wrangle whose reckless pursuit of his own ends will determine all their fates (just as Dyer once did), the attempt and thwarting of a desperate bid for freedom, and the argument for free will in an uncontrollable universe.

The climax of Conflict #3 is going to throw back the veil and reveal in vivid, concrete terms the themes this writer has come here to explore.

Development

Now that they're hooked on Conflict #3, the reader reads the Conflict development, how that hook scene builds upon itself, continuing to reveal and intertwine hidden aspects of all the elements introduced in the Hook, Conflict #1, and Conflict #2 (and always aiming toward the whole point of Conflict #3, which is going to kick the characters right in the teeth). Just as in the earlier episodes, this occurs in a series of one to three conflicts, which may be longer or shorter, depending upon the length of the story and intentions of the writer.

In *Thieves*, Bowies admits to Keechie that two Laws were killed in the shoot-out at the accident after their last bank robbery, and she knows Chicamaw's the one who killed them. Keechie's father tells the newspapers Bowie's kidnapped her, and Bowie decides to send her home. However, before he does, he, Chicamaw, and T-Dub rob one last bank, where T-Dub is killed, Chicamaw injured, and T-Dub's new young wife arrested. Bowie is the only one who escapes, accused in the newspapers of being a dangerous outlaw aided and abetted by a mysterious woman. Bowie, terrified and humbled by his close brush with disaster, promises Keechie never to see Chicamaw again.

In "Dwarf," Ralph goes away for a minute and comes back looking pleased with himself. Through the intense loneliness of

Development

the carnival crowd, the Dwarf appears, heading toward the Mirror Maze.

In *Postman*, this is where it gets complicated. Frank and Cora are interrogated by the DA, who bullies Frank into signing a complaint against Cora for his injuries so it won't appear he killed the Greek for the insurance (which Frank has never even known the Greek has). Frank gets a lawyer then, who arranges for Cora to confess to his own assistant posing as a fake detective in order to get it off her chest so she won't panic in front of the judge, then pits the insurance companies against each other, forcing them to collude in self-protection because the Greek had three policies in effect at once—one almost expired and two new ones overlapping that particular week.

In *Riders*, Faye's mother dies, and Faye comes to live with Withersteen. Venters returns from Surprise Valley and confronts Tull over stealing Withersteen's cattle, and Tull, in revenge, sends his right-hand man, Jerry Card, to steal Withersteen's prize horses, killing one of her riders in the process.

In *Otranto*, Matilda meets Theodore in person, they fall instantly in love, and she sends him to hide in the forest. There he stumbles across Isabella and valiantly hacks the daylights out of her father Frederic in her defense when Frederic appears in disguise to rescue her. Dangerously wounded, Frederic gasps out his identity and the prophecy against Manfred. Frederic is conveyed to the castle, where he recovers.

And in "Norderney," the Cardinal tells the story of "The Wine of the Tetrarch," in which St. Peter is so obsessed with his own reaction to the crucifixion he's unable to help a stranger with a mysterious spiritual burden.

Now the characters are showing things they're made of through aspects they never even knew about themselves, and that revelation of *what they're made of* is the heart of everything the writer has to say about being alive.

Act II: Conflict #3 climax— *Second Plot Point*

Now we're reaching the whole point of Conflict #3, which is the story's *second Plot Point*.

The reader has become addicted to this story through the build-up of Conflicts and is gradually succumbing to the complexities of the plotline. Up until now, they've thought they could keep things straight and even guess where it's all going. After this, they have no idea what the writer has in mind.

Yep, *we* know where it's going. It's going toward the whole point of Conflict #3, the climax, which is that second Plot Point that's going to spin them like whirligig bugs, completely altering all their preconceptions about what they want and how to get it.

But first. . .

Faux Resolution

That build-up takes a heart-moving detour at the last minute and the characters fall into the faux resolution of Conflict #3. *The saints have arrived!* It's a happy story, after all!

In *Thieves*, Bowie and Keechie are settled down in a sweet little cabin in a small town far from anywhere, finished with their lives as bank robbers. Keechie is relieved that they're not going to Mexico, and Bowie says he's decided to hire a lawyer to rescue Chicamaw from the death sentence, although he

Development

reassures Keechie he still won't see him. They'll stay quiet, straight, and safe.

In "Dwarf," Ralph waves the Dwarf into the Mirror Maze for free, assuring Aimee he's being benevolent, just as she's always wanted him to be.

In *Postman*, Frank is released without prosecution, and Cora is acquitted when the insurance companies refuse to testify against her. And just when Frank and Cora think it can't get any better, the lawyer hands them the insurance check from the insurance company that has agreed to act as figurehead—ten thousand dollars (in 1934!).

In *Riders*, Lassiter discovers Venters and Bess, happy and in love, in beautiful Surprise Valley.

In *Otranto*, Theodore reveals the story of how he came to Otranto, an honest man on a noble mission.

And in "Norderney," the mysterious stranger of the Cardinal's story reassures St. Peter he, too, will probably be crucified, if that's what he hopes for, his moral soul saved.

This faux resolution is more profound than the last, not just a quick glimpse of a dream but a three-dimensional revelation of what would make these characters truly happy. The reader identifies with these characters now, and this beat draws them fully in emotionally. Now the reader *longs* for these characters to find their happiness.

Climax

Finally the reader reaches the whole point of Conflict #3, which is that second Plot Point—the other huge event that spins the characters' story and sends them flying off in an even more unexpected direction, that deadly direction they didn't see coming but should have, their heads whirling until they just about snap off their necks—the climax of Conflict #3.

In *Thieves*, it's Christmas Eve morning when Bowie's and Keechie's pipes freeze and they have to call in a plumber. When the plumber behaves suspiciously, they realize he's going to turn them in to the police for the reward, and they leave their sweet little cabin without packing—suddenly they're on their way south in the direction of Mexico.

In "Dwarf," the Dwarf goes to his regular room in the Mirror Maze and begins to scream and scream, and when Aimee arrives she realizes the mirror has been altered to make him look even shorter than he really is—suddenly Aimee realizes, after he's already done his damage, that Ralph is heartless and cruel, and she has no hope of ever reconciling him with the Dwarf.

In *Postman*, the lawyer says he wants the ten grand. No, he only wants half. No—there's a brief resolution at the last second, when he laughs and says he won't take any of it, he's just tickled to death that he pulled such a good one over on the DA he hates—suddenly the seeds of doubt are sown in Frank's and Cora's minds and they know they have no hope of trusting *anyone*.

In *Riders*, Venters chases down Card in another hellbent-for-leather, rip-snorting chase scene, cornering him on the stolen Wrangle on the edge of a cliff. Wrangle, who's lost his mind in the intensity of the chase, must be shot. And when Venters finally succeeds, Wrangle falls over the cliff, taking Card with him—suddenly both Withersteen and Tull have lost something of huge importance, and they have no hope of avoiding a cataclysmic show-down.

In *Otranto*, Matilda and Isabella square off over Theodore, whom they both covet. Hippolita, attempting to reconcile them, advises Matilda to marry Frederic as Manfred desires, and Isabella, appalled at the idea, tells Hippolita Manfred

Development

intends to divorce *her*—suddenly they all become aware that they have no hope of escaping futures that have been decided for them by others in exactly the wrong way.

And in "Norderney," the Cardinal's story ends on the revelation of the mysterious stranger as Barabbas, who was crucified alongside Jesus—suddenly the characters realize nobody is what they seem and we have no hope of designing our fates for our own purposes, not even to save our souls.

Wow—Act II has brought us so much to *work with*. We must give it our undivided attention, perform our analysis upon it, take our long, involved notes. Examine exactly how Act II has turned into a revelation of the characters and their story. They've confronted their fears, the obstacles to their hopes and dreams, and revealed the deep significance of their themes.

But their stories *still* haven't been resolved.

We're approximately $2/3$-$3/4$ of the way into this story, and the reader's reeling.

So the writer can switch tactics.

Chapter 22

Climax
Holographic structure, Act III

Act III: Faux Resolution

Whee, doggies! We're done with Act II and suddenly, *unexpectedly* being slipped into Act III.

We've passed the second Plot Point, the characters' trajectories have shifted once again, even more significantly, and all our hair is standing on end. The reader doesn't know up from down anymore, and this new switch in tactics keeps them completely off-balance.

And (again, you say!) we're at a hook, this time the hook of the Faux Resolution, which is going to culminate eventually in the whole point of the Faux Resolution, its climax: the utter relief of everyone involved, that point in the story at which the characters (and reader) believe they've actually gotten out of facing their worst nightmare.

And the first bit of *that* hook is the *hook scene*.

And the very first words—those few reassuring words that pull the reader in and make them want to read the next words—that's the *hook sentence*.

Hook

Hook sentence

In *Thieves*, a lawyer's house is described as both straight and a little warped, next to a church (subtle irony).

In "Dwarf," Aimee turns on Ralph in tears.

In *Postman*, all in one sentence, Frank and Cora put the insurance money in the bank, buy lots of flowers, and go to the Greek's funeral (which just happens to be occurring that day — but the whole business with the complicated insurance maneuver has the reader's head buzzing so hard they never even notice this coincidence, which allows the writer to keep the tension at a singing peak).

In *Riders*, Venters rides defiantly through town leading Withersteen's recovered horses.

In *Otranto*, Jerome, reunited with his beloved son, interrogates Theodore about his escape from Otranto.

And in "Norderney," the young man gets up to change the tallow in the candle, as it goes into its death throes (again — subtle symbolism).

Hook scene

In *Thieves*, Bowie and Keechie meet with the lawyer, who says he can keep Chicamaw from getting the death sentence and also pass Bowie's money on to him so Bowie won't have to see him. The lawyer invites them to eat Christmas Eve dinner with him and talks through the whole meal with real insight about the economic conditions that create a climate of bank robbery, blaming the wealthy. Bowie agrees that capitalists are "thieves" just "like us."

In "Dwarf," Aimee asks Ralph what's wrong with him, how he could do such a thing to the Dwarf, and runs away from him without waiting for an answer.

In *Postman*, Frank and Cora attend the Greek's funeral, amid whispers of who they are and how the Greek died.

In *Riders*, Venters announces to everyone on the street that Card is dead, a message for Tull. One of Withersteen's riders tells Venters he's seen Lassiter in the bar with Oldring, so Venters—in a rage—goes into the bar, announces he's there for vengeance on behalf of Bess, and kills Oldring, only puzzled that the last look in Oldring's eyes is of love and his last words an unfinished sentence about Bess.

In *Otranto*, Theodore admits to Jerome that he lied to Manfred about how he escaped Otranto in order to protect Isabella.

And in "Norderney," the young married couple lies down in the hay together holding hands and falls asleep while the madwoman and Cardinal sit awake.

As always, we must be aware of what goes into the *hook sentence* and what illumination reveals in the full *hook scene*. You'll see how the clues to conflict in these hook scenes of the Faux Resolution relate to the climaxes of the Faux Resolution, now eerily like the stories' Climaxes, only their opposites: Bowie and Keechie agreeing on the necessity of springing Chicamaw from prison and escaping south, Aimee defending the Dwarf, Frank and Cora coping successfully with the aftermath of the Greek's murder, Venters and Lassiter gunning down their enemies, the thwarting of Manfred, and the uniting of the hearts of the Cardinal and the madwoman.

The climax of the Faux Resolution is going to resolve the characters' surface dilemmas, laying the groundwork for the contrast between that and their real, underlying nightmares, which brings all the viscerally vibrating threads of the story into the same frequency at the same moment.

Development

Now the reader is hooked on the Faux Resolution, and, full of relief and new-found confidence, they read the Faux Resolution development, luxuriating in how that hook scene builds upon itself and finds ways to *appear* to resolve all the aspects of the story and put out the burning fuses, subtly drawing the reader's attention away from the real danger ahead (and always aiming toward the whole point of the Faux Resolution, enticing the reader to look completely the other way). Just as in all the previous episodes, this occurs in a series of one to three conflicts, which may be longer or shorter, depending upon the length of the story and intentions of the writer.

In *Thieves*, Bowie and Keechie settle down in New Orleans, within a safe distance of the Mexican border, and Bowie reads in the paper that Chicamaw's trial is over and he's escaped the death sentence.

In "Dwarf," Aimee finds her way out of the Mirror Maze and begins searching the carnival for the Dwarf. She feels numb—not angry at Ralph anymore, not shocked or frightened—just numb.

In *Postman*, although they should now be happy, the tension of what they've been through is too much for Frank and Cora. Cora leaves town, and Frank's solution is to take up with another woman, who invites him to go with her to Nicaragua to catch pumas. He almost goes with her—but in a brilliant one-liner realizes Nicaragua won't be far enough away.

In *Riders*, Venters learns from Bess that she was not Oldring's involuntary wife but his daughter, whom he loved. Meanwhile, Lassiter tells Withersteen Milly was not his wife but his sister, so Lassiter is free to love Withersteen. And Withersteen swears to Lassiter she loves him (although he doesn't believe her because she faked her fondness for him when she first knew him).

In *Otranto*, Hippolita fails to get permission from Jerome to divorce Manfred, as he desires, a solid win for Isabella and the others.

And in "Norderney," the madwoman and the Cardinal exchange profound insights as the young people sleep, realizing they understand each other in a way nobody has ever understood them before.

The characters are managing not to face their nightmares here. They don't believe they *can* face their nightmares. And *what they don't believe they're made of* is the other side of the portrait their writer is going to such long and meticulous and heartfelt lengths to draw.

Act III: Faux Resolution climax—*Feinting*

So we're reaching the whole point of this Faux Resolution, which I've described as the story's *Feint*.

The reader has been soothed by the build-up of this Faux Resolution and deeply reassured that *they know* where it's all going.

Oh, yes. *We* know where it's going. It's going toward the whole point of the Faux Resolution, which is suckering the reader into believing exactly what they now hope to believe. And that will set up the greatest possible contrast between that enormous relief and the knock-out blow of the Climax.

Climax

But first...

Anti-Faux Resolution

...something tricky. Instead of a faux resolution to give the reader a chance to take a breath between conflicts, as in all the previous faux resolutions, this time there's an *anti-faux resolution*—the opposite of a breather, a little poke with a sharp stick to make sure the reader's still awake. It ain't over 'til it's over. *You there!* Sit up!

In *Thieves*, Bowie learns from a newspaper that Chicamaw has been sent to the deadly prison farm in Texas.

In "Dwarf," The owner of the shooting gallery runs up and says the Dwarf has stolen one of his guns.

In *Postman*, after Cora gets home, the lawyer's fake detective/assistant tries to blackmail them with her confession.

In *Riders*, while Withersteen and Lassiter are arguing over whether or not she really loves him, little Faye is kidnapped.

In *Otranto*, Manfred convinces Frederic to agree to a double wedding between Frederic and Matilda, Manfred and Isabella, causing blood to drip from the marble nose of the statue of Alfonso at the mere thought.

And in "Norderney," the Cardinal admits to the madwoman that he is not the Cardinal at all, but the Cardinal's assistant, who killed the Cardinal so he could take his place.

This beat throws the reader for a loop, because the writer has conditioned them through the three-time repetition (remember that humans resonate deeply with threes) to expect relief at this point. But it's not relief! It's the opposite! *What?*

Suddenly, the reader doesn't know which way to turn.

Climax

And finally the reader reaches that whole point of the Faux Resolution, which is the point of total surrender — the opposite of the up-coming Climax, that point at which the characters (and reader) truly believe the nightmare has been avoided — that clever Feint, the climax of the Faux Resolution.

In *Thieves*, Bowie talks to Keechie, who hasn't been feeling good, about going to Mexico, finally convincing her it's the only place they'll be safe.

In "Dwarf," Ralph has cornered Aimee back in the Dwarf's room of the Mirror Maze. She realizes she has no feeling for Ralph anymore and turns to leave.

In *Postman*, Frank beats the lawyer's assistant to a pulp and gets the confession away from him.

In *Riders*, Lassiter goes to the Mormon church and shoots Bishop Dyer dead, telling him he knows Dyer is the one who ruined Lassiter's sister Milly, kidnapped her little girl, and has now kidnapped little Faye, and declaring Dyer won't destroy the lives of any more young girls.

Lassiter reveals to everyone that Bess is the little girl kidnapped long ago from his sister Milly and proves Oldring was not Bess's father but the man to whom Dyer gave the child. Dyer and Tull intended Oldring to raise Bess as a rustler and break the heart of Milly's husband — Tull's old antagonist back home, from whom Tull kidnapped Milly to bring her to Utah at Dyer's bidding. However, Oldring came to love Bess and raised her as his own daughter, educating and protecting her, foiling Tull's revenge — all of which Lassiter learned that day Withersteen's rider saw him with Oldring in the bar, right before Venters killed Oldring. Now Withersteen gives Venters and Bess her prize horses so they can escape Utah (and the Mormons) forever.

Climax

In *Otranto*, Hippolita shuts everyone up by docilely taking Manfred home with her.

And in "Norderney," the false Cardinal asks the madwoman if life has any more purpose than to smile at the Devil. She agrees that this is a great art and the purpose of life. Then she demands he kiss her so she will not die unkissed, and he kisses her.

Oooh, the Faux Resolution is a marvelous twist in the story. We must be sure we understand exactly what's going on here and why. Examine how Acts I and II have been brought to their culminations and then suddenly, adroitly, turned inside-out.

The Faux Resolution is the point at which so many aspiring writers think they've finished writing their stories. They think they're done.

They're not done.

Now is the moment for the characters to *stop* showing what they're made of, to take a break, to collapse and let their weakness and wounds and lack of capability be fully revealed. That lack of capability is what spells their downfall.

We're approximately $5/6$-$7/8$ of the way into this story, and the reader's a complete, unsuspecting innocent.

So the writer can sock it to them.

Act III: Climax

The stage is set. The characters are poised. All of this long, involved story, all of those complications, all of that deep, wonderful, rich development—and we're ready for the real reason we're all here.

So, of course, we're at a hook, this time the hook of the Climax, which is going to culminate eventually in *the whole point* of this *entire story*.

And the first bit of *that* hook is the *hook scene*.

And the very first words—those few electrifying words that pull the reader in and make them want to read the next words—that's the *hook sentence*.

Hook

Hook sentence

In *Thieves*, Bowie tests a pen in order to write a letter to the lawyer.

In "Dwarf," Aimee catches sight of Ralph in the Dwarf's mirror.

In *Postman*, Cora announces to Frank that she's going to turn her confession over to the police.

In *Riders*, Withersteen's prize horses carry Venters and Bess across the sage.

In *Otranto*, Manfred realizes Jerome knows Isabella loves Theodore.

And in "Norderney," the madwoman gracefully lifts the hem of her skirt and hands it to the Cardinal.

Hook scene

In *Thieves*, Bowie sends money to the lawyer to buy a faked bench warrant and sheriff's badge for Bowie, who feels obliged to break Chicamaw out of the Texas prison farm before he's killed there.

In "Dwarf," Aimee can't stop staring at Ralph in the mirror.

Climax

In *Postman*, Cora explains she's confessing to the police because she wants to see Frank hang, knowing she can't be found guilty of a crime for which she's already been acquitted. It turns out the woman with whom Frank almost went to Nicaragua has shown up looking for him.

In *Riders*, Tull and his men chase Venters and Bess, so Bess gives her horse its head and in another fabulous chase scene proves to Venters she's the best rider out there on the purple sage. Having outrun Tull, they pause together at the sound of bizarre thunder coming from the high canyons around Surprise Valley.

In *Otranto*, Manfred worries over Theodore's striking resemblance to the portrait of Alfonso.

And in "Norderney," the sopping hem of the madwoman's skirt proves the flood has reached them.

Now for the last time, we are aware of what goes into the *hook sentence* and what is illuminated in the full *hook scene*. The clues to conflict in these hook scenes of the Climax relate, finally, to the climaxes of Climax. Bowie struggles against all odds to satisfy both his loyalty to Chicamaw and his love for Keechie— resulting in the destruction of all three. Aimee and Ralph face the truth about who he is—a man with a stunted soul. Frank and Cora can never be together—although they truly love each other. Venters and Bess, Withersteen and Lassiter, must all escape Utah and the Mormons—before they are destroyed by Tull. Manfred faces his prophesied doom— and is undone by Theodore's rightful claim to the Castle of Otranto. And the Cardinal and the madwoman face the awful mystery and majesty of life and death simultaneously—both together and alone.

The climax of the Climax is going to *catapult the reader into epiphany.*

Development

So here the reader is, thoroughly hooked on the Climax, with the entire story dragging behind it like a burning fuse. The reader reads the Climax development—by now simply unable to stop—and discovers how that hook scene builds upon itself, revealing the story in ways the reader never expected, while scaring the pants off them and making it appear there is really, truly no way out of this utter catastrophe (and always aiming toward the whole point of the Climax, which is *proof* that there's no way out). Just as in all the other episodes, this occurs in a series of one to three conflicts, which may be longer or shorter, depending upon the length of the story and intentions of the writer.

In *Thieves*, Keechie learns she hasn't been feeling well because she's pregnant and finally agrees to go to Mexico with Bowie, and Bowie, in a harrowing scene, finally manages to free Chicamaw from the prison farm in Texas.

In "Dwarf," there's no room for development scenes—it's all fast as a sledgehammer at this point.

In *Postman*, Frank convinces Cora he loves her, and she breaks down and admits she loves him back. The two of them, crumbling under the pressure, lie awake nights wondering how Frank is now going to kill Cora so she won't turn him in. Eventually, they confess everything they've been through to each other, swear they love each other, and Cora tells him she's pregnant. She insists he *prove* he won't kill her by giving him a perfect chance.

In *Riders*, Withersteen and Lassiter ride into the high canyons in search of Surprise Valley. However, partway there Lassiter tells Withersteen he has to confront Tull and his men, who are now following them, and as she waits for him she hears a terrible shoot-out.

In *Otranto*, when Bianca screams that she's seen the giant's hand on the stairs, Frederic calls off the double wedding. Manfred, overhearing Theodore in a love tryst and believing Theodore's beloved to be Isabella, stabs the woman and manages to kill his own daughter, Matilda. Everyone stands around her shrieking and wailing as she dies.

And in "Norderney," the madwoman and the Cardinal gaze at the sleeping young couple on the brink of death.

Now the characters are beginning to face their nightmares. Not the full extent yet—the writer saves that for last—but a taunting, terrifying, foreshadowing of their nightmares in the final conflict of the Climax, which sets up one final, overwhelming visceral vibration inside the reader, who begins suffering bodily symptoms of stress and euphoria. The reader is no longer just hooked in the gut. They're not even emotionally invested.

They're *trapped*.

The characters (and their reader) are going into a state of literary psychosis in which they're no longer able to distinguish between reality and surreality. *They don't know what they're made of anymore.* And it is by detaching them from reality that the writer prepares the reader for epiphany.

Act III: Climax climax—*the Whole Point*

So we've reached the whole point of the Climax. This is the grand finale.

The reader has been shocked, startled, and eventually petrified by the build-up of this Climax, unable to live now without finally learning where this whole story's been going all along.

We know where it's been going all along. It's been going toward the whole point of the Climax, which is *the whole point of the entire story*.

But first...

Faux Resolution

That build-up takes one last detour that dupes the reader one last time into believing the Climax has come and gone, the nightmare has been averted, and the characters have survived unscathed. It's the faux resolution of the Climax. *Thank your lucky stars!* We escaped just in time!

In *Thieves*, Bowie anxiously but safely returns from breaking Chicamaw out of the prison camp before Keechie wakes from a nap, and Bowie promises he'll never leave her again. Chicamaw is free, and they're just across the border from Mexico. *They're going home.*

In "Dwarf," Ralph turns to see what Aimee's staring at. *They're about to be reconciled.*

In *Postman*, Frank and Cora get married, then swim far out into the ocean so he can kill her if that's what he intends, and Frank realizes how much he loves her. He dives deep and feels everything being cleaned from him, leaving only his love and their future. *Everything becomes clear and beautiful.*

In *Riders*, Lassiter returns to Withersteen, injured but safe, with little Faye, whom he has taken back from Tull. They arrive in Surprise Valley. *They've made it.*

In *Otranto*, Manfred at long last repents of his evil ways. *Evil is conquered.*

And in "Norderney," the madwoman stops the Cardinal from waking the young couple, telling him when she was young she aspired to live so that no birds were ever again confined in cages. *Life is a vision of freedom.*

Climax

This beat is the full development of the joyous face of the story's theme. Freedom! Reconciliation! Virtue! Beauty! The reader thinks they've finally found what they came for.

They haven't found it yet.

Climax

And here the reader is at whole point of the Climax, which is *the whole point of the entire story*.

In *Thieves*, Just as Bowie is getting up to fetch Keechie something to soothe her morning sickness, the two of them are shot down in a burst of gunfire. This is described immediately afterward in a newspaper articles as the righteous end of a manhunt for the dangerous bank robber, Bowie Bowers, and his armed girlfriend—thereby making society safe from "thieves" like them.

In "Dwarf," Ralph sees that he has turned into the Dwarf in the mirror—he has become what he has mocked.

In *Postman*, Cora thinks she might be miscarrying, so Frank in a panic rushes her toward a hospital, but in a single, brief scene he wrecks the car and kills her. He is convicted (in one sentence) of murdering both the Greek and Cora for the insurance money and given the death penalty—and in the very last sentence of the very last page he unexpectedly breaks the Fourth Wall and asks the reader to pray that he and the woman he loves wind up after death in the same place.

In *Riders*, Lassiter must roll Balancing Rock across the entrance to Surprise Valley in order to cut off Tull, but at the last minute he can't do it. He knows once he has there will be no way out and the three of them will be trapped forever. Only Withersteen's passionate declaration of love and insistence finally decide him at the very bottom of the very last page, and he rolls the rock, causing an enormous avalanche to rain down on Tull—the thunder Venters and Bess paused for as they escaped Utah.

In *Otranto*, The ghost of Alfonso appears, finally freed of his marble statue. There is a long and involved Resolution, in which Alfonso names Theodore his heir, Manfred confesses that his grandfather poisoned Alfonso and faked his will so his own heirs could inherit the Castle of Otranto, and Jerome explains that before Alfonso died he married a young Sicilian woman, who gave birth to a daughter, who was Jerome's wife and Theodore's mother. Manfred, exposed, abdicates in humiliation, and Theodore marries Isabella, although he will always be in love with the dead Matilda—a black-humor, gothic resolution to a gothic comedy.

And in "Norderney," Dinesen reveals that dawn is breaking, throwing bars (subtly like a birdcage) across the loft, and—at this moment when the madwoman is about to tell whether or not her life has been worth living—Dinesen uses the cliffhanger technique of her idol Scheherazade to illuminate the inherent precariousness of human life, just as the false Cardinal and madwoman have spent all night illuminating it, by *refusing to tell*.

That epiphany belongs to the reader.

Chapter 23

More Climax
Confronting the pirate

Pin-Pointing Your Climax

Suppose we're working intensely on an *incredibly* deep and meaningful story.

We're not us, we're an eighteenth-century American writer, maybe, who's been to Europe and is now on the way home, so we have to do this work on shipboard. But that's okay because we're so completely immersed we could work on it anywhere. Or else we're a European who's been to America. Or an Asian who's been to South America. Or an Indian who's been to Asia. Or an African who's been to Antarctica—but anyway, we're on a ship, working, working, working away as towering waves crash over the prow and the tang of salt wafts to our nostrils.

News of this extraordinary story has leaked out into the general public. Since we have a huge international reputation as a storyteller, everyone knows this story is worth a fortune. It's rumored to be the pinnacle of our career. It's the most amazing production of a genius brain, which has already produced stories more memorable than Cervantes', plot twists more baffling than Shakespeare's, audience investment more powerful than Homer's. Anyone who possesses this story will be richer than Croesus.

It is—as Bertie Wooster would say—a real *pip*.

But of course we keep it top secret so no one can steal it.

Then *disaster strikes*. Oh, no! Our ship is hailed and, in quick order, boarded by pirates. They hog-tie everyone on board and take command. We are hauled up in chains before the pirate captain, the notorious Assuipe, with his reputation for collecting strange and unusual treasures and selling them to buyers of enormous wealth known only to him.

And he wants our story.

"No!" we cry. "I won't tell you! I'd rather *die first*."

Unfortunately, he's okay with that.

In an instant, his minions have flung out a plank, and we are encouraged at sword point to climb up on it and begin our promenade. They're leaning over the side of the ship tossing edibles to attract sharks.

"Well?" he calls when we're a third of the way along.

"I won't!" we yell furiously over our shoulder, rattling our chains above our head.

Poke, poke go the points of the swords.

"What do you think?" he calls when we're two thirds of the way along.

"Never!" we bellow, yanking futilely against our chains. One foot slips, and we jerk it back with a private whimper.

Poke, poke go the points of the swords.

"It's time, matey. Will you tell me, or won't you?" he calls when we get to the end of the plank.

"No!" we cry passionately from the very depths of our heart.

The pirates lift, and the plank begins to tip. Below our feet, shark fins are circling. The tang of salt wafts to our nostrils.

We shriek. "It's—!"

What?

Making a Scene Out of Your Climax

So we're sitting at the table in the captain's cabin across from Assuipe, guzzling a flagon of wine and trying not to bang our elbows on the brass table rail that keeps stuff from flying off during storms. He's allowed us to change our britches, but we're still wondering whether our heart will ever stop pounding.

Probably not.

"Tell me again," Assuipe says, clutching his quill and preparing to write laboriously as we speak. He's not very literate.

"It's the story of a genius of a writer," we say wearily, "whose greatest idea, the most extraordinary premise, the pinnacle of a brilliant career, is stolen by a—a pirate."

"I like it!" Assuipe belches into his fist. "Go on."

"It starts in a little seaside village where the writer lives. She's down in the waterfront pub with her best friend, Panther Jack—"

"Screw that," says Assuipe. "Tell me about the pirate who steals the idea."

"No, that's at the *end*." It's obvious Assuipe knows nothing about storytelling. What a cretin. "First I have to tell you the story. See, Panther Jack is this kind of maverick sailor. She could be a ship's captain, she's so experienced, but she's not into power or authority, so instead she roams the seas on whatever adventure strikes her fancy. She and the writer grew up together—"

"Screw Panther Jack," says Assuipe. "I want to hear about the pirate."

"Could you *stop* interrupting? I'm trying to tell you—"

"About a pirate."

"*No.* The pirate's not even *in* most of the story. He only comes in at the very end. And, anyway, he just wrecks everything. He's just part of the premise. He's not what the story's about—"

"I like him." Assuipe grins, and we immediately wish he hadn't, because his teeth are the worst. "Your premise is the whole point of your story. *Bozo.*"

"—so the writer goes overseas, and while she's there the pattern of everything she's been through crystallizes in her mind, and—*bingo!*—Panther Jack's story comes back to her, and she realizes it's the kernel to the most brilliant premise—"

"—which *is* that a terrible and swashbuckling pirate king steals a stupid story so he can live happily ever after—" Assuipe is trying to massage the cramp out of his writing hand.

We shake our head. "Living happily ever after isn't part of the premise. It's the resolution to the Climax."

Assuipe sighs and puts down his quill. "Living happily ever after is the Resolution to the *story*. But before that, the resolution to the Climax is me letting you get down off that plank." He hawks and spits into his empty flagon. "You know, for a famous writer, you sure don't know squat about structure."

Romeo & Juliet, Climax

faux resolution scene

The star-crossed teenagers have planned to meet in secret immediately after they're married. The girl and the priest who married them have come up with an elaborate plot in which she fakes death to escape her family so she and the boy can run away together. The only thing left to do is tell the boy.

The girl drinks the potion and falls into her drugged sleep. When she wakes, she and her young husband will be reunited, and they'll be free.

That's the *faux resolution* scene of the Climax.

climax scene

However, the boy arrives at the girl's tomb ahead of schedule and finds her apparently dead. In his horror and anguish, he pulls out a bottle of poison and drinks it. The girl comes to shortly after that, finds him draped dead over her, and in *her* horror and anguish pulls out his dagger and stabs *herself* to death.

That's the *climax* scene of the Climax.

After that, the priest rushes in just in time to not save anybody.

He's the *resolution* to the Climax (which is not the same as the Resolution to the story—you notice a minor resolution is so fleeting it can be tacked onto the end of the climax scene).

Down curtain.

The Idiot, Climax

faux resolution scene

The man finds his rival, an old and close friend, with the woman they both love. The man's friend has become increasingly deranged throughout their mutual courtship of this woman, even to the extent of threatening to kill the man, who is an epileptic and a kind of saintly fool. He loves the woman partly because she's a fallen woman who needs his empathy. Now she has first agreed to marry him and then run off with his friend yet again, leaving him at the altar.

The man chases the woman and his friend and finally catches up at his friend's house, where he's sure they can all be reconciled.

That's the *faux resolution* scene of the Climax.

climax scene

The friend shows the man the woman's dead body. In his anguish over breaking the heart of his best friend, the saintly fool, he has killed her.

That's the *climax* scene of the Climax.

They cower together in their mutual despair.

That's the *resolution* to the Climax.

Down curtain.

Emma, Climax

faux resolution scene

The meddling young woman has managed, through her incessant interference, to prevent a friend from marrying the man who loves her. She's also managed to get herself proposed to by the last man she would ever marry and to act the dupe for a couple hiding their engagement from their elders. She has, in her frustration over constantly screwing up, been inexcusably rude to a woman of much lesser advantages.

Now she is on her way to meet the man she loves, joyfully unaware that, through this final screw-up, she has alienated his affections.

That's the *faux resolution* scene of the Climax.

climax scene

The young woman's beloved scolds her roundly for her behavior throughout the story, and she realizes she's been completely wrong about everything.

That's the *climax* scene of the Climax.

She has an epiphany about who she is and what her life is all about.

That's the *resolution* to the Climax.

Down curtain.

Anna Karenina, Climax

faux resolution scene

The Russian aristocrat who has left her husband and son for her lover looks one final time to her friends and lover to pull her out of the spiraling depression into which she has fallen after the birth of her illicit daughter. However, they can't save her from herself.

She realizes in a flash of epiphany it's up to her to resolve her tragic life and goes alone to a train station to think.

That's the *faux resolution* scene of the Climax.

climax scene

The woman, distraught, listens to people talking around her and, little by little, comes to see her life as a complete sham. She decides quite rationally to kill herself, carefully times the passing of a train, and throws herself under its wheels.

That's the *climax* scene of the Climax.

All light goes out — she is dead.

That's the *resolution* to the Climax.

Down curtain.

More Climax

"The Legend of Sleepy Hollow," Climax

faux resolution scene

A man competing with a more successful, more rakish, generally more likely suitor for the love of a young woman learns at a party that the woman appears to have chosen the other man. He leaves for home feeling rather downhearted but not defeated. He has faith in himself. And nobody's won the young woman's heart yet.

That's the *faux resolution* scene of the Climax.

climax scene

On the way home, the man sees the headless horseman of legend riding toward him. Panic-stricken, he tries to out-run the ghoul. He is heading for a bridge, thinking if he can get across it he can make it home safely. He comes to the bridge, and the figure *throws its head at him*.

That's the *climax* scene of the Climax.

This Climax has no *resolution*. (It's a ghost story.)

Down curtain.

Identifying the Crux of Your Climax

The problem most writers run into is that their best moment *isn't their Climax*.

Because what interests them most isn't what they thought would.

We *thought* we wanted to write a story about teenage love that proves youngsters must abide by the wisdom of older and cooler heads. But you know what really got us? The boy hiding in the girl's garden to stand under her balcony. It was too much for us! And the girl leaning over the rail of her balcony under the stars to the sight of his beautiful face in the dusk below? We didn't plan on that. But, wow, does that scene throw off *sparks*.

So by the time we get to the premise, the reader's thinking, *Tell me more about that fascinating scene when teenage love catches fire.*

This is probably the biggest reason people pants. Because they don't want to get to their planned Climax and discover they've come all that way for nothing.

But it's not for nothing! Oh, no. It's all part of the work. We would never have figured out about the balcony and the garden if we hadn't gotten ourselves thoroughly involved in these characters' world, if we hadn't been in there wandering around, following them from place to place, spying, eavesdropping, taking notes as fast as we could. If we hadn't been asking ourselves, "But what about this angle? What about that thread? Where is this going? Where has that been?"

We might have wandered right past the girl and boy flirting under cover of night and never given the import of that scene another thought. "Minor scene. Useful only for moving characters from one point to another. Nothing to notice here. Carry on."

This is why I tell writers to identify first their protagonist's *needs*. Two mutually-incompatible needs. The needs that drag them into this story.

Because the *choice* between our protagonist's needs is the ultimate nightmare they must eventually face.

Juliet needs to obey her parents. She's a young teen, docile, intelligent, *cultured*. Her parents' whims are her commands. And this is fine so long as she never needs anything else. But then one starry night hormones appear in her world in the figure of a beautiful, poetic young man her own age, and suddenly Juliet is trapped between her awakening passion and painful denial, between obedience to and rebellion against those under whose authority she lives. In a story of *love*. And *survival*.

That makes the Climax of her story the moment in which she must choose between her beloved and her life.

Romeo also needs to obey his parents. He's also a teen, and although he longs to be level-headed in the heat of anger he is volatile enough to kill. And when he falls in love with Juliet and kills her cousin Tybalt in a fight over her, he too becomes trapped in this story of passion and denial, of obedience and rebellion. Of *love*. And *survival*.

That makes the Climax of his story, as well, the moment in which he must choose between his beloved and his life.

Which makes the two of them simply fabulous co-protagonists for this heartwrenching drama.

So we work with our protagonists until we know—as deeply as we know ourselves—exactly what they need and how they manage to thwart that need. Then we imagine any number of situations that might force them to choose between those opposing needs, and we select the one that affects us most powerfully. Our Climax.

We won't write it yet.

Building Total, Complex, Shocking, & Inevitable Significance into Your Climax

We've got a Climax in mind. It's not our original idea. No. We just used that to point the cannon in a likely direction so we could climb in and fire ourselves off. We went flying over the landscape, and the further into this fictional world we got the more of it we saw, the better we understood it, the clearer became the forces that make it what it is. And at some point we saw the apex of the whole thing.

There it is. This is what we were after all along.

It appears right after things seem to have finally all settled down.

And it's *fabulous*.

Oh, we want to write it. We're climbing over our own head to get at it. *Everything's there*.

But wait.

Because a Climax needs to be the culmination of the entire story. And how do we know what that culmination is until we've written the entire thing?

Not only does the Climax hold our premise, it also holds everything most essential and fundamental to our protagonist and main characters. And not just what we assumed was most essential and fundamental to them when we first met them, either. Not even what we figured out it was after we'd spent a lot of time hanging around with them. Not even what they told us, secretly, deep in their hearts, when nobody else was listening, as we contemplated together the ruin of their lives.

Even more than that.

As we write a story—what pantsers love about it—things crop up. Things we never saw coming. And, as Flannery O'Connor pointed out so many years ago, certain of these things keep coming *back*. The more times they come back, the more varied the situations in which they appear, the more meaning they begin to acquire in and of themselves. They take on resonance. By the end of the novel, they have become symbolic.

These could be objects. Or images. Or sounds. Or mannerisms. They could be certain colors, certain

More Climax

environments, certain memories, certain conclusions that certain characters keep finding themselves drawing about different circumstances. They could be mysterious triggers. Mysterious people.

A carved button. A blood orange. The call of an osprey. A finger on a collarbone. Someone in a trenchcoat on a bicycle. Waves battering at the brassy base of a cliff. *I turn inside-out all I love best.*

We won't know what these symbols are until we've worked ourselves deep into the heart and soul of every single scene, traveling alongside our characters through all of the trauma through which they must go. We can't see those symbols from up high. We have to get down inside the scenes and live them. Everything is there, and we're looking only for the most striking, pertinent, unique details out of everything, and when we've listed them, considered them, fingered them, and finally included them, they begin very...slowly...to accumulate.

So that when we write the climax scene to our Climax, the one big scene it's all about, we need that accumulation of significant details at our elbow to go through for *only the most significant and telling.*

And we don't have the whole accumulation until we're done with every other scene.

Not only that, but out of that accumulation, chances are the details that are going to hit our reader the hardest in the Climax are the ones so subtle they haven't made hardly any appearances yet.

Oh! The secret fuse burning away underneath it all!

Yes.

So we save the Climax. We take notes on it. Add questions. Scrawl comments on the backs of envelopes. Fill page after page of ideas and thoughts and ruminations and meanderings. We interview our characters. Stage conversations between them that they could never hold in the course of the plot. Let the detective sit down with the murderer and share a flask of rotgut and hash out some of the more important details.

"You were there?"

"Behind the door. You never even knew."

"That's going to affect my investigation—"

"That's probably when I dropped that slip of paper."

"You think?"

"I imagine. Because you had to get it before I threw the sailor out of the dinghy."

"That's right. And *that* didn't happen until after Mariah called the watchmaker."

"Of course! Which is why the watchmaker *already knew* about the *drop*."

Eureka!

I was working with a client one day on a Young Adult (YA) fantasy novel. We'd done great work on a scene the week before, in which one character charges to the rescue of a friend in a lake, throwing up a huge, dramatic splash of white water against the night. It was a great moment. A *great* effect.

My client came in the next week saying, "You know that scene we wrote last week? Yeah. *Huge hole.*" And he reminded me that the character who charged to his friend's rescue is deathly afraid of water.

Rats. So we sat down and talked about that. And we decided it's perfectly possible to lose our head and charge straight into a phobia in the defense of someone we care about if our adrenaline gets up suddenly and we truly believe our friend is in mortal danger. Sure, it is! But afterward?

More Climax

Well, it just so happened we'd planned for a scene after that particular subplot in which the friends all have personal meltdowns and go their separate ways (setting them up for the Climax). And what plugs into the need for a meltdown better than having just gotten ourselves totally immersed in our worst phobia?

Accidental motivation—there it is!

We must let go the reins and let our subconscious work. There's so much in there we can't pry out with a crowbar. We must immerse ourselves in our fictional world, write scenes around and about our characters, see what floats to the surface.

When I was in high school, I had a teacher who loved the word 'serendipity.' She talked about it all the time for most of a year. She was obsessed with the concept of how things can just *happen* to occur and it turns out they fit together like the pieces of a puzzle.

Those flashes of insight are the layering that makes a Climax shocking.

Shocking, as well as *inevitable.*

Chapter 24

Layering Plot
Believable fiction II

So now we come to the most complex, authentic, essential aspect of structure: **layering**.

Novels are long. Series are even longer. And in this day and age, when such gorgeous works as Jean Rhys' *Wide Sargasso Sea,* Joseph Conrad's *Heart of Darkness,* Virginia Woolf's *To the Lighthouse,* and John Steinbeck's *Tortilla Flat* simply aren't good enough for us, because they're — by golly — less than 70,000 words, even a short publishable novel is by definition longer than most of the great novels in our literary canon.

All of which means that now, more than ever, we need layering.

Plot layering is using one or more subplots and a whole handful of plot threads to string out the action and deepen the significance, dragging our reader along through hundreds of pages and tens of thousands of words by the very scruff of their neck, never once losing our grip on them or letting them glance — however momentarily — at the clock.

Without them, the reader is simply too likely to look up and realize they have their own life to live.

We must prevent that from occurring to them.

Layering Plot

Main plotline

All stories have a main plotline: the fundamental struggle inside the protagonist between their two conflicting needs. This is what we talk about when we talk about the basic progress of a story from Hook through Development to Climax. This is what our story *is*.

We've discussed the main plotlines of each of these stories in detail: the tragic love stories of *Romeo & Juliet*, *Wuthering Heights*, *Dolce*, and *Anna Karenina*; the tension-packed adventures of *Thieves Like Us*, *Dark Passage*, *The Postman Always Rings Twice*, *Heart of Darkness*, and *Riders of the Purple Sage*; the tragicomic escapades of *The Castle of Otranto*, *The Violent Bear It Away*, *Henderson the Rain King*, *Little Women*, and "The Aspern Papers"; the profound insight of "The Dwarf," *The Fountain Overflows*, *The Brothers Karamozov*, *The Idiot*, and "The Deluge at Norderney."

When we examine the ways in which plots are structured, paced, and interwoven, we must be aware of this. We must always be watching for hints to subplots and plot threads in them.

Everything swings from the main plotline like a braid depending luxuriously from one lush head of hair.

Subplots

Subplots come and go throughout a story. They interact with the main plotline. They help develop character traits, illuminate motivation, and focus the driving fuel of the main plotline. They even appear at crucial moments, such as the climaxes of each episode, to bolster and cast into relief the main plotline, adding to its power.

When we're designing a climax for an episode of our main plotline—the climax to a Hook, Conflict, Faux Resolution, or Climax—we need all the *oomph* we can get. So we coordinate at least one subplot to reach a climax at the same time. We start the climactic scene in the main plotline, do a quickstep into a subplot, maybe throw in a subtle plot thread, and end on the main plotline again.

This forces a single scene to serve more than one purpose at once. That's scene-level layering.

And in this way the climactic scene is multiply gripping, the reader's visceral investment in the story stimulated by the depth of following more than one plotline at once, while also satisfied by the resonance of the main plotline within the scene itself.

The key to using subplots is to remember they are *always* subservient to the main plotline.

When the beloved cousin Rosamund of Rebecca West's *The Fountain Overflows* is haunted by the poltergeists who apparently operate on her father's behalf, that isn't the main plotline. The main plotline has to do with the childhood of the protagonist, of which Rosamund is the pivotal secondary character.

West needed Rosamund and her mother to move in with the protagonist's family, and she needed them to have a tragic and even dangerous other life that would never allow a reconciliation with Rosamund's father that might remove Rosamund from the protagonist's family circle. So at the climax of Conflict #1, West sent the protagonist and her mother to call on Rosamund and her mother and thereby witness the violence of the poltergeists in person. The next thing we know, Rosamund and her mother have moved in, and the story has gained its essential secondary character.

Layering Plot

West could have used any number of pressures upon the characters to accomplish this goal, and she could have told her story without any such goals at all if she'd really wanted to. It would still have been the story of the protagonist and Rosamund. It would still have ended in their arrival at the threshold of adulthood, facing the inevitable Climax of the paths upon which they've walked throughout all their years together.

But the story would have been missing that layering, that complexity that contributes so much to the realism of what West wanted to explore.

It's *vital* to distinguish between the story we really mean to tell and the subplots that add and contrast to it but are not the story itself. Sometimes these things can become confused, and the writer winds up writing a story quite different from the one that leads to the Climax inherent to the personality of their protagonist.

We know, of course, that we need more than one story: a main plotline and a secondary plotline running alongside it. That secondary plotline is our main subplot. But it's not the only subplot. And it is *not* the main plotline.

West constructed her story around the premise: what if an ordinary girl and an extraordinary girl grew up together? What would happen when they stood on the threshold of adulthood and the ordinary girl was forced to face the inexplicable extraordinariness of her dearest companion?

West's main plotline is the childhood story of the ordinary girl. Her main subplot is the childhood story of the extraordinary girl. And her minor subplots add to both.

Rosamund's story could not be told without the protagonist's. But the protagonist's could—if necessary—be told with some character other than Rosamund.

And any time the minor subplot of Rosamund's dreadful father and the threat of paranormal tampering ceases to add to the main plotline, all of that sinks out of sight for awhile. Then when that minor subplot is needed again, the father reappears—until he eventually reveals himself as a musician so consummate it brings tears to the eyes of the protagonist's concert pianist mother.

"Why?" She is devastated by the knowledge of his beautiful talent coupled with his cruelty.

He has no answer for her and in this way adds to the tragic undertone of the story, the sense of growing danger on all sides in this otherwise fairly ordinary and yet exquisitely-rendered childhood.

A subplot is *always* subservient. It must *always* serve the forward movement of the main plotline—as must even the main subplot, as it crashes against the main plotline over and over until it alters that story into something it has never been before.

Subplots are not the braid itself—they are the locks of hair from which the braid is woven.

Plot threads

And then there are plot threads, those zillions of minor moments that appear and disappear like fireflies in the night.

Plots threads are different from subplots in that they're not major storylines running along concurrent to the main plotline. But they're different from simple scenes in that they're capable of moving from scene to scene, appearing more than once as the story progresses.

Plot threads not only add to the significance and interest of each subplot, pacing themselves perfectly to lull whenever the

Layering Plot

subplot lulls, to build whenever the subplot builds, and to peak whenever the subplot adds its weight to a climax in the main plotline. They also create delicate rhythms of their own, so that plot threads are used by the most adept to toy with the reader's mind and develop complex beats and back beats so minor they can only be felt—like the high notes of a dog whistle—by the sensors of the subconscious mind.

When Francis Tarwater catches a ride to the city with the salesman Meeks in Flannery O'Connor's *The Violent Bear It Away*, it's a tragicomic episode in which Tarwater reveals for the first time in interaction with another character the many facets of his suspicious and ignorant mind in almost equal measures, to the accompaniment of Meeks' own questionable grasp on reality.

Yes, O'Connor needed to get Tarwater from his greatuncle's remote cabin (now a smoldering wreck) to the city where his only other relative lives. That's how this plot thread adds to the forward motion of the main plotline. But she didn't have to do it this way. She could have managed without this scene at all and still told her story just as well. And Meeks goes away after this. We never hear from him again. We do hear from other characters who play his role in Tarwater's life—strange and sinister characters without roots in the main plotline whose sole purpose is to drag Tarwater from pole to pole of his journey, until one of Meeks' prototypes finally leaves the young man passed out and robbed by the side of the road.

Riding with strangers is a plot thread—a vivid series of moments in the telling of this story that illuminates a plethora of miniscule shining details about the characters and their setting, giving the reader their money's worth as they ride the avalanche of this wonderful story.

As with subplots, the story could survive without these plot threads. But it wouldn't have the complex layering of a truly complete work.

And as with subplots, plot threads accomplish all their subtle purposes while *always* simultaneously forwarding the movement of the main plotline.

Plot threads are not the locks of hair—they are the shining individual hairs that make up each of the locks of the intricate braid we're weaving.

Without subplots and plot threads, we can still have a head of hair. But what we do with it...*aaah*. That's storytelling.

Chapter 25

Epiphany
Beyond holography

You know what I love about the Internet? (Not everything, by any means.) I love that I can get nostalgic over a silly 1969 movie that thrilled my soul when I was a young teen, and look it up and—hey, presto!—there it is.

If It's Tuesday, This Must Be Belgium.

I saw that dippy movie in the early seventies, probably the very summer my family returned from an endless nine-month tour of South America and Europe in a modified Land Rover named after a dog. I was thirteen, romantic, anxious to finish growing up and become a cute hippie. *Seriously* out of touch with reality.

That movie could have been made just for me.

What I did not realize was that movie *wasn't* aimed at young teen travelers abjectly grateful not to be stuck in a car with their siblings anymore. This honestly never even crossed my mind. It was aimed at *older* teen travelers who had—*en masse*—suddenly in the late sixties 'discovered' Europe and European hostels (much the way Europe 'discovered' America a scant 475 years earlier), along with the idea you could dash wildly around the planet on a schedule to make a double-

Epiphany

booking dentist blush, trying to see the world without ever stopping long enough for the world to see you.

Well, we were young.

And the only reason I know all this as well as I do is that I eventually returned to Europe. Having had world travel, dim and smoky hostels full of painfully attractive older teens, and the sight of Europe passing through a car window in an unidentified blur all embedded in my developing adolescent DNA, I had no choice. I had to get back to my roots.

I was thirty by then—still too young to afford decent hotel rooms, but now too old to join those wonderful teens over whom I'd originally swooned. I had five weeks to see everything from England to Italy, three of which I spent in a youth hostel in London playing pool with Australians.

I'm telling you, I *was* that movie. When I got home, reeling and dizzy, exhausted and twenty pounds thinner and stone-cold broke, I was in love.

I went right back to Europe as soon as I could afford it and started interviewing for jobs. I actually had two job offers as a tech writer in London but got hung up in Immigration. I toyed with the idea of joining the expatriate writers' community I heard was springing up in Prague the summer after Czechoslovakia split.

Instead I got laid off from my dreadful job tech writing at IBM and went to Australia to visit the Australians I'd met in London (a whole other kettle of fish).

But I left a part of me behind in Europe. That footloose, artistic expatriate life had been my destiny.

You see, I'd known about it since I was a young child. I have an aunt who had been a starving artist on Paris' Left Bank in the 1950s, running around the rainy, cobbled streets barefoot at night, tossing her long hair and laughing her cackling laugh, romancing and being romanced under the street lamps.

I was going to be her. I knew that fantasy life was out there, just beyond my fingertips. It was *waiting* for me. *In my bones, I knew...*

And this is exactly how we want our reader to feel about our story.

We want to give them characters within a hair's breadth of their fondest dreams of themselves—mistake-addled, misguided, and tormented maybe, but also intriguing, heart-breaking, witty, and, at long last, profound—who live in the one place they miss most in all their lives—the summer they were nineteen and lived in a shack on the beach, the winter after their divorce when they learned to night ski in the silent forests of Vermont, the evening they suddenly realized in a blinding epiphany what black holes are and why you don't want to be an ant crawling around the rim of one.

We want to give our reader, as well, the fantasies they've had of living places they've never lived, of having adventures they'll never have.

We want to take them wholly and completely into these characters' worlds: into the minutiae of telling moments, the details branded on the retina in an instant of passion, the tactile experience of being alive—being alive—just being alive.

We want to reach into their dreams and pull something out that's still tied to them by the heart-strings. We hold it up and turn it under the light:

"It's beautiful. It's devastating. It'll eat you up and spit you out, make mush of your brains and liquid of your soul. It'll be around the globe three times before you even know what direction it's gone, and you'll spend forever chasing after it."

We show it to them. *"It's your life."*

Part 2
Revision

Chapter 26

Writing & Rewriting with Franz Kafka
Do-It-Yourself editing

Franz Kafka lived and died an unknown. Although his stories are so vivid and philosophically brilliant the adjective 'kafkaesque' has become a part of our language, Kafka himself labored in obscurity.

A German-speaking native of Prague, he grew up in the Jewish quarter of Prague's medieval Old Town at the turn of the twentieth century—an era that meant for Kafka less the rise of Jewish self-awareness or political unrest or even Modern fiction than the rise of *bureaucracy*.

He worked throughout his short life as an insurance company paper-pusher, resulting in his unfinished masterpiece, *The Castle*, with its dreamlike exploration of the constant fruitless motion of red tape, its nightmare quality of endless, struggling stasis. A novel of the most bizarre non-story, *The Castle* follows the adventures of Kakfa's hapless protagonist known only as K. from the moment he arrives mysteriously in a nameless village at the foot of a domineering castle—much as Prague, that most lovely of European medieval cities, lies across the Vltava River from Prague

Castle—and begins his hopeless, utterly determined quest to gain entrance to "the Castle" for no particular reason.

Many years ago, I visited Prague. It was the winter Czechoslovakia split into the separate countries of the Czech Republic and Slovakia, and I was so utterly innocent of political events I was surprised to learn from a fellow tourist on the train leaving the city that my Czechoslovakian money would be worthless within 24 hours.

It was *cold*. I slid down Petrin Hill on ice through the trees, crossed the *art nouveau* Čech Bridge over the Vltava River, and walked the cobblestone streets of Old Town in a euphoric, shivering haze. I climbed the historic clock tower on Prague's medieval Old Town Square (with its magnificent astronomical clock) and photographed a 360-degree panorama of the city—all those mysterious, winding little streets, all those huddled, misshapen, tiled rooftops, the magnificent bulk of the castle like a dragon on the horizon.

A dream landscape.

And there's no question Kafka wrote about it as a dream. *The Castle* begins pointlessly, proceeds through innumerable meaningless obstacles whose importance can be determined solely through the seriousness with which the characters take them, culminates in no actual progress whatsoever, and accomplishes, in the end, nothing.

Kafka had no visible plan, no structural goals, no inevitable Climax in mind (although we can extrapolate what that Climax could have been based entirely upon the needs of his poor protagonist, so abundantly clear and powerful).

However, it's almost impossible not to feel ourselves, as we read, in Kafka's place, hunched over his papers evenings and weekends outside his dull work hours, recording with feverish intensity his protagonist's unbearably tangible world. It's the same feeling behind Mervyn Peake's *Gormenghast* trilogy—that of a genius of observation working at the height of his power to get down in excruciating detail an alternative universe as real as our own. There's the very strong impression that obsession with the meticulous is what kept this writer *alive*.

Although Kafka's story is twisted to serve a philosophical function far beyond that of storytelling—a darkly-comic illumination of bureaucracy as a lifestyle—it is that white-hot passion for noting the moment-by-moment experience of living that makes his fiction sing. And even more vitally, among his papers after he died were discovered not just the manuscript of *The Castle* but numerous variations on that manuscript: an alternate beginning, a continuation beyond the ending, countless fragments, excised scenes and paragraphs and phrases, rewritings and reworkings of events, characters, and developments. Some of the excised episodes go on for thousands of words.

The same story told over and over again, in every permutation and detail its author could possibly imagine.

This is the nature of fiction, writers, this multiplicity of storytelling. Truly, our first draft is barely a fleeting glimpse of the story we really mean to tell. It is only after we've waded in over our heads and rooted ourselves in an unshakable perspective upon our characters' experiences that we can begin the real work of recreating those experiences for our reader.

Kafka died of tuberculosis at the age of 41, barely published (his masterpieces unrecognized and unknown), a man who'd spent his life agonizing over whether or not to marry a woman he wasn't certain he wanted to marry (who wasn't certain she wanted to marry him), his amazing intelligence wasted on bureaucratic paperwork, finally at long last in love, the day after the father of his young beloved refused him permission to marry her.

We all seek in fiction some euphoric release from the drudgery and heartbreak of daily life. We open ourselves to our imaginations, writing and rewriting and rewriting yet again, inserting and removing scenes, paragraphs, episodes, and lines. And it is through this repetitive, painstaking process—over and over—that we find ourselves immersed in our unique, detailed, and yet utterly *real* fictional landscapes. There is no avoiding boredom and agony, but there is this temporary, ephemeral escape.

We are all Kafkas at this work.

Chapter 27

Vision & Revision

The story you need to tell

We have come *so far*.

Remember way, way back in the early days, when we talked about the difference between character arc and narrative arc? Remember how we talked about who we are, just solitary, individual human beings having ourselves some needs, forming ourselves some opinions, following our agendas wherever they happen to lead us, as we wander around out here on the surface of this planet our whole lives through? Remember being a noun? Remember having verbs?

Let's walk back through our story together now with all that teeming beneath the surface of everything we've written, and we'll re-envision the original vision that first lead us to these iridescent shores.

Rethinking Motivation for Character Arc

Cause-&-effect. Needs. Choices.

The things that make us human.

We've created a protagonist with two or more intensely powerful, intensely conflicting needs. Those needs have forced this protagonist to behave and speak in quite specific ways.

And the ways in which they behave and speak have created for them a variety of situations that, once they were in them, they desperately wanted out of, situations they couldn't get out of without making things immeasurably worse.

We've put that protagonist in a room or garden or culvert or on a street or island or mountain or under a thundercloud or tent or blanket with some other characters, who also have their own needs.

We've thrown in a stick of dynamite and leaped out of the way to see what would happen.

And it was *brilliant*.

We kept this up for a good, long time, until that protagonist's conflicting needs collided in a life-changing shower of fireworks and we forced them to choose.

And eventually, footsore and weary-worn but with a gleam of well-earned satisfaction in our eyes, we've fetched up here alongside everyone else in Revisionland. We're a bit surprised to see the others looking *quite* so footsore and weary-worn. But we're gentle souls and would never dream of mentioning this. Not out loud, anyway.

Now we've taken a big, full, satisfying rest after all that hard work, and we're ready to get back into our story, to begin the second phase: revision.

So the first thing we're going to do is take out a notebook and ask ourselves, "How well do I know this protagonist?"

And we're going to dig for the answer—to that and to a few other pertinent questions.

What is this protagonist's primary overwhelming need? I know we wrote this down way back in the beginning and stuck it up on post-it notes over our desk (*you didn't?*), but I want to ignore that at this point, and we'll apply ourselves solely to the protagonist in the Climax that we so recently and brilliantly wrote. We'll pretend that Climax is a short story (flash fiction even), and we've come to it cold without knowing any of the rest of this story exists. We'll put on our thinking caps to analyze what we get out of reading that Climax as though for the very first time.

What's the *fire* in this strange new protagonist's belly, the death-defying drive that makes them forge straight into that Climax and fight there tooth-&-nail for everything they love and believe in? What makes this protagonist *go*?

We'll write the answer at the top of a fresh page of a notebook.

We'll draw a box around it. Spend some time inking in the lines of the box, making them thick and dark and really remarkably straight. Doodle in three-dimensional sides for the box. Add shadows. And dents. And cracks. And travel stickers. Add a cat sitting at a distance with one of those inscrutable cat expressions, not saying or even thinking anything, just looking at it. That's the witness.

Got it?

Good.

Now, what deep inside this protagonist is pitted *against* them in that Climax? Not external forces—internal. What do they love and believe that's irreconcilable with their first need? What's the equal-but-opposite fire in their belly in this Climactic scene that's *fighting back*?

Remember to focus only upon the climax scene of the Climax.

We'll write it down on the middle of the page below the box we just drew. Decorate it with its own little box, its own light and shadows, its own dents and cracks, its own evidence of having traveled a long and painfully difficult road. If the first cat is looking too directly at the first box, we'll give this one a cat of its own. Otherwise, one cat will suffice.

Got it?

Good.

We'll doodle some lightning bolts between the two boxes.

Now we'll ask ourselves, "Exactly how could these two needs have gotten this protagonist into this dreadful calamity?"

We'll take copious notes on this, fleshing it out as fully as necessary. We won't re-tell the story. We'll forget we ever even *knew* that story. We're not looking for surface issues, we're diving beneath the wave, re-envisioning the story from a completely different perspective. This is essential in order to know that the story we've told is, in fact, the story we meant to tell.

We'll ask ourselves, in all honesty, "What do you suppose *happened* here?"

Then we'll ask ourselves, "*And how could these needs have led somewhere else?*"

We'll write about that for awhile.

We'll draw circles and brackets around especially important points as they come up in our notes or as we notice them afterward, using arrows and asterisks, scribble little comments to in the margins about things we forgot to mention. We'll fill up pages. Keep our hands moving. (When we scratch our cheeks, we'll try not to draw on our own faces.)

We'll always be wondering, "What do those two needs imply about this protagonist? How could my character have responded to their problems differently, given their fundamental, driving forces?"

We'll write sideways on the pages if we feel like it. Write at an angle or in loops or upside-down. Write in a fake accent, if it helps. Nobody's ever going to see this stuff. (By the time we send it to someone like me, it'll be all cleaned up and back in its public disguise again.)

Then we'll ask ourselves, "What would have been the perfect compromise to this Climax, the best possible way for a protagonist with these particular needs to convince themself they weren't going to have to choose between those needs after all?"

It doesn't need to be a scene or even an event. Just an idea, a possibility—some way for them to wriggle out of their nightmare right before it happens.

We'll deliberately avoid thinking about the original solution to their dilemma. If we can't avoid it, we'll think about its opposite. Pose the question as if for the first time ever.

We'll take notes.

And we'll keep in mind that a Faux Resolution is a negative Climax—where the hook of a Conflict or Climax is jarring, the hook of a Faux Resolution is soothing; where the conflicts of a Conflict or Climax are increasingly full of conflict, separated by momentary lapses only to catch the breath, the conflicts of a Faux Resolution are increasingly resolved solutions separated by momentary lapses, one at least of which pokes the reader out of their comfort zone; and where the faux resolution of a Conflict or Climax is a clear, kind, writer-to-reader respite, the anti-faux resolution of a Faux Resolution is a *bear*. That makes the climax of a Faux Resolution a truly *fake* resolution.

We'll create a diagram for the relationship between the Climax as we have newly perceived it and the Faux Resolution we've just illuminated, a flowchart or family tree sort of thing, tracking our protagonist with their burning internal fires from

271

the Climax backward into the effects that caused it, all the myriad possibilities branching off in all directions.

Think about how many second or third or fourth cousins we must have who have never even dreamed of our existence. There are simply dozens of distant cousins to our protagonist's choices populating the parallel universes of the story inside our imagination.

We must ask ourselves what they are.

We'll continue to back up all the way through this story in this manner, working backward from the Faux Resolution through Development, addressing each Conflict as it comes up.

We'll always keep in mind as we do so: what does this protagonist need? and what else do they need? and how does the mutual incompatibility of those two needs keep banging them against themself, striking sparks?

And what if *something else* happened instead?

We'll uncover the hidden aspects of our protagonist's internal conflict. and record them in great, whacking, glorious detail.

Eventually we'll arrive at the Hook and write long and copiously about that. And finally—sprawling all over the pages of one full notebook or more—there will be a whole multitude of deep, intricate roots to this Climax, as developed backward through the Faux Resolution and Conflicts and Hook and as defined through the lens of our protagonist's internal conflict.

Take a long breath and admire it. You had no idea a story contained such *depth*, did you?

Then we'll go through it all slowly and thoughtfully, doodling circles or boxes or pyramids or stars (we can use different colors, if we like colors) around only those most special, magical roots at each, separate layer, the ideas with the freshest, most amazing potential.

"She remembers the abyss between her parents." "They're forced to collude against their will." "It becomes clear they've made a terrible mistake." "He begins to fight back against himself, but in a funny way." "She first intuits that it's not going to work."

It doesn't matter how many there are. All we care about right now is that they're different, surprising, *magical*. And it doesn't matter where they might lie in relation to the scenes we've already written. Some might be spot on, and some might be a million miles away. It's okay. We're not outlining something we've already outlined before—we're searching for those hidden potentialities that vibrate with the greatest possible tension and significance.

We'll know them. They'll make our fingertips tingle when we pass our hands over them.

We'll copy them onto a fresh sheet of paper under their headings: Hook, Conflict #1, Conflict #2, Conflict #3, Faux Resolution, Climax. The most special, magical roots of character. We'll dink around until we know they're right.

We'll make sure, as we group them under their general headings, that they increase in tension from Conflict #1 to Conflict #3, from beginning of the story to the end. Then within each general heading, we'll number them in order of increasing tension.

Now we'll take out *another* fresh sheet of paper (you didn't know revision took so much fresh paper, did you?) and draw a sweeping curve skewed toward the far end, and letter in extremely small letters each of those special, magical roots in chronological order according to their numbers and general headings, beginning at the Hook and finishing at the Climax.

There.

Our protagonist's real character arc.

Reorganizing Events for Narrative Arc

This is retro-design. And once we have our protagonist's fresh character arc all laid out before us, we can use it to determine the real story, the real series of scenes buried inside our first draft.

We have a character arc tracing the path of a series of essential elements of character development, leading the protagonist from the moment in which life first conspires to force them to change, all the way through that change, to the point of tossing the reader unexpectedly off the rainbow at the end of that protagonist's change.

Which point I like to consider the *ex*-change.

We've explored and solidified the character development of the story, both reaffirming those choices that gave us our first draft and discovering the new and deliciously unexpected aspects our first draft is meant to discover. And now we can see it—the beauty of the geometry.

So we're examining our Climax and how it serves the purposes of our protagonist's character arc. They've reached some nightmare moment in which they can't possibly meet *both* their fundamental, driving needs. Is this really the event they were headed toward all along? Did something extraordinary occur along the way that sent them somewhere else— someplace far more earthshaking, more illuminating of their nightmare? Someplace that makes their choice between needs even *more* agonizing?

It should be right there in our notes.

We'll hunt it down, purse our lips over it, and put the end of our pen thoughtfully to our nose.

Is that it? The *real* premise?

We'll think about it for a long time. We'll search our notes for alternatives, scribble our latest, most exciting flashes of intuition, tap the end of our nose as we think. (Stick out our tongue as far as we can to prove no one's watching.)

We'll take as long as we need for this part. Hours, days, weeks, months. Truly...what's it all about?

Eventually we'll know—the *real* event that crowns this story.

Got it?

Good.

We'll take a fresh notebook and write at the top of a fresh page in our best calligraphy, "Once upon a time..." and fill in our real premise, the event we've come so far to create. It's fine if we've already created it. It's fine if we haven't. We'll keep it in one sentence, just as we've done before when we discussed premise and Climax.

Once upon a time...

Our best calligraphy.

If we screw up the calligraphy, we'll tear off the page, wad it, throw it over our shoulder, and write our premise again on the next page. (Try not to do this more than once, though, because some poor tree did have to *grow* that page.)

Take a good look at it. Isn't it *lovely*?

Now we'll read back through the elements of our protagonist's character arc that appear under the Climax. Add to that list the alternatives to our premise that we've just discovered. Shuffle them around until they're in increasing order of tension. Think about some perfect little faux resolution event to that Climax—an instant in which our protagonist

275

believes they've just slipped in under the wire. Put that where it belongs. It's okay if right now there's more than one choice.

We don't need to add these to our clean sheets with our best calligraphy. Just have them jotted down in our notes and clearly identified for later.

Then we'll read back through the elements of our protagonist's character arc that appear in our notes under the Faux Resolution. They're in chronological order, yes? And within the context of the Faux Resolution, we can tell which element carries the most punch, the one this Faux Resolution is all about, yes? That's the climax to the Faux Resolution—*yes?* We'll play around with them until we're certain that's the best Faux Resolution for this particular Climax. Think up new ones. Let our intuition explode like fireworks.

Now we'll imagine (or track down) an event in which that momentous element would be best illuminated. Maybe we've already written it. Maybe we haven't.

We'll write it—again in our best calligraphy—a few lines below our premise on the same page. One sentence. Some event to reassure our protagonist in their most vulnerable hour they will not after all be facing what, in fact, we know they will.

It should be a negative version of the premise directly above.

Beautiful.

We'll continue now to back up through our protagonist's character arc identifying the most devastating change under each of the three main Conflicts. We'll picture for each one an event in that Conflict that would best illustrate the trauma that creates that change. Maybe that scene is already on paper. Maybe it's not. Maybe it's somewhere in our notes, maybe it's in our journal, maybe it's been set aside in our imagination, or maybe it's simply never *occurred* to us before now. We'll write a one-line description of each of these three scenes (one for the climax of each Conflict) with utmost elegance below the other, spaced every few lines down the page below the Faux Resolution. Just a scene, an event, a moment in all eternity to illuminate the corresponding step in the character arc, a moment after which our protagonist will never be the same again.

"*She remembers the abyss appearing between her parents* — they were making hand-cranked ice cream." "*They're forced to collude against their will* — they reach a point on the glacier where they can't go forward and they can't go back." "*It becomes clear they've made a terrible mistake* — she admits to him the giraffe was a bad idea." "*He begins to fight back against himself, but in a funny way* — he develops an aversion to his own hair." "*She intuits it's not going to work* — she breaks her own heart over the costume."

If we simply can't decide between more than one, we'll write both.

Again, we'll take a really long time over this. Days. Weeks. *Months*. Although it involves such minimal actual writing, this phase is a *huge* amount of the creation of story. And it takes a profound inner connection to our guts, to our subconscious understanding of this protagonist and this particular change in their life — to this story. That kind of profound connection takes a long time to grow from seed and even longer to foster to full maturity.

Eventually, after we've worked our way backward through all three Conflicts, we'll arrive at the bottom of the page, and there we'll sit, staring at those final elements of the character arc that appear under the Hook on that long skewed curve across our character arc's pristine page. These are the most fundamental aspects of our protagonist's personality. We may or may not find them familiar. Whatever they are, it is the combination of them that makes our story absolutely necessary to write. We'll find the one element there under the Hook that causes the greatest curiosity in the reader. Ask ourselves whether or not that element is something new that's just now ready to surface from our subconscious. We'll allow to swim into in our mind some vision of some event that would be simply the most thrilling, most illuminating event with which to open such a heartwrenching narrative.

"The avalanche first separates them. Or she races the train until she's hit. Or he runs down the street until he finds the unlocked door. Or the stranger knocks at the window."

We'll take several long, luxurious breaths to steady our hand.

And we'll write a brief description of that scene below all the others. *Our best calligraphy.*

We'll sit back then with a sigh and contemplate this page. Appreciate it. Luxuriate in it. Think about framing it and hanging it on the wall over our desk. Ask ourselves whether or not we'd need to re-paper the wall in order to bring it out to greatest effect.

We'll read this list through, bottom to top, in a gentle, sonorous voice, running one finger tenderly up the page past each element as we read until our finger comes softly to rest at the very top. The end. We'll lay our palm flat on the page when we're done. Feel how that series of events encapsulates the change in our protagonist's life.

These are the essential elements of our story's narrative arc.

Re-ignoring Theme through Tao

Remember when we talked about the Taoism of theme? And I neglected to say exactly what's so Tao about forgetting about it?

That, my friends, is *Tao*.

The mystics claim the less we know about Tao the better we are at it, which means since all I know is that one little epiphany I'm practically an *adept*.

It's an epiphany that will take us everywhere.

The first real novel I ever completed was about love. *Awww.* That one got me through eight years of higher education.

The next novel I completed was about death. *Ooooh!* That one got me through the last sorrowful years before my grandfather eventually faded away.

I was working on that second novel in the early nineties at the same time that my closest writing friend was trying to break into Regency Romances, and she asked me one day to help her identify her 'themes' according to the rules of the Regency people. Her themes were, not surprisingly, mostly centered upon love.

"I try not think about theme too much," I told her. I'd explained about approaching Resolution mystically, like the White King, as though it weren't there. "I explore what I want to explore. I've written one novel about love and another about death. The only thing left for me now is *taxes*."

Virtually everything we can discuss about writing fiction is craft: character, plot, structure and development, techniques and details and holistic understanding.

And yet the purpose of fiction, when all is said and done, is art: flinging the reader into an epiphany at the core of the universe of themself, a flash of insight that makes their own world and experience of life greater and more meaningful *because* it is their own.

Only the light we shine on the iridescent underbelly of our story, in the final analysis, turns out to be the illumination of our themes.

Chapter 28

Reshuffling Your Deck
Revision

Now, if you're anything like me (and every serious writer I've *ever* known), at this point you're just about ready to settle for those two pages of arc for your entire story and go on with your life. All that *work*. All that *time*.

We're not getting any younger.

However, if you're still anything like me (and every serious writer I've ever known in my *entire* life), at some point in the future you're going to pause in the middle of whatever you're doing and wonder, *But how would it have turned out?*

When nobody's looking, we'll be back in front of those two pages of arc with a pen in hand, and we'll be hearing voices coming toward us out of the distance, through the paper. The voices of our characters.

And we'll begin the revision.

Brainstorming

The first thing we'll need to do is review exactly what our story is. We'll pull out our two beautiful pages of paper with the character arc and narrative arc all spelled out for us.

Reshuffling Your Deck

We'll read them through cold to see if we can raise goosebumps on our arms. If we can, good. We're ready. If we can't, we're in luck. We've got notes.

We'll go through our notes—all those notes we took in the revelation of the real character arc and narrative arc, as well as the notes we took throughout the writing of the first draft—and explore exactly what we discovered when we wrote them. It's very possible we didn't notice the core of our story when we were in the heat of writing about it. Even if we did, this is the time to make sure we knew what we were talking about.

Then we'll do some number-crunching on our first draft—all those scenes we've written, developing our own voice—to determine how many words we tend to average per scene, and we'll make notes to ourselves beside every step of each element in our new narrative arc on whether we'll use one or two or three scenes for each step.

We'll make some comments to ourselves about what goes into those scenes and how they cause their own chronology, how they build on each other, each leading to the next step.

We'll develop a symbol to mark which scenes have already been written (and where in our manuscript they are right now).

And we'll spend some time writing fresh notes on individual scenes or sequences of scenes.

Overall Organization

Then we'll set up the organization of our new draft. We'll take a bunch of paper or open a fresh, untouched document on our computer, and we'll sketch out this new organization we've designed. Leave the notes we just assembled separate. They're not the new draft. This is.

I like to break my new draft up into separate documents for separate chapters. Or else I break it up into the six basic elements of plot structure with a narrative arc of chapters within each element. Sometimes I even create a document for each scene in a chapter, all the documents in one folder.

No matter what, I never write a full draft of my manuscript in one document. I need to bring the document down to a manageable size, otherwise it gets too large and becomes a *total* nightmare to navigate. There's time to put everything into a single clean document in the very end, when it's in its final polished draft.

Once we have the documents, we can insert a line describing each element and each chapter, in order—even each scene, if we've got it. So we know what goes where.

Lots of blank, empty, innocent space in between the labels.

Scene-by-Scene Arc

Now we'll take our first draft and cut it up scene-by-scene, dropping each scene where it belongs in the fresh draft. This can take a really long time and become *really confusing*. So we'll keep the notes we assembled handy as we move back and forth between our first draft and our fresh draft. Double-check a lot. If we scramble the organization at this point, we'll wind up writing a whole other story from the one we intend.

We'll keep a list at our elbow to keep us oriented toward the Pole Star of our Climax.

We'll flag scenes yet to be written in something that leaps out at us—like fire engine red.

Reshuffling Your Deck

Intuition

Now we get to the weird part.

We're going to take off our jacket or overshirt, roll up our sleeves, remove our shoes, and climb on our desk or table. Move breakables out of the way.

We'll very carefully climb into the first document. Sit down in it. Gaze around. Get used to being there.

Now we'll move slowly and with great sensitivity on our hands and knees from the hook of this chapter or episode, through the development, to the faux resolution and climax, feeling as we go for irregularities.

We'll move back and forth. Search for holes in logic, cracks in character, inessentials. Eliminate scenes and feel the result. We'll move things around if we like. Use our antennae. We're building in tension toward a faux resolution and, ultimately, life-changing climax.

When we can close our eyes and move through that document from hook to climax without looking, and it all makes beautiful, crazy sense, we'll pat ourselves on the back. Then we'll climb out of that document, shake the kinks out, and move on to the next document.

We'll progress through all our documents. This will take a very long time, but when we reach the point of beautiful, crazy sense in each one it will be like bathing in warm, fragrant oil. We'll use our most obscure muscles. Set our nerves alight.

We'll feel our heart when we've finished them all. Does it feel good?

We're probably ready.

Fun

We're going to choose a scene somewhere in the early middle of our story and sit down to write. We can use fresh paper or a new document if we like. We can cut-&-paste this scene into place later. Whatever we do, we won't pressure ourselves.

This part is a bit like going into labor. Prodromal labor is a nightmare and produces absolutely nothing, so don't go there. We'll relax, kick back, pat our stomach.

Breathe.

When we begin to visualize our characters in some particular scene (or anywhere—maybe we accidentally chose a different scene to start with), we'll go ahead and start recording them in words. Long, luxurious, way over-the-top detailed words. First the hook of the scene, aimed at the first conflict. Then the next and the next. Maybe unexpected conflicts, maybe ones we've planned, but always moving toward the climax we've decided is *exactly right*...and after awhile our contractions will begin. (And they'll be a whole lot more fun and exciting than *real* contractions, I can guarantee.)

We'll sink in up to our eyeballs. Feel it through our whole body. Feel the shiver of excitement. We're writing again!

Scene after scene after scene, we're back in the saddle. We thought we'd never get here again, and yet *here we are*.

Don't worry if it takes a few scenes to fully make the transition out of the planning part of the brain and into the writing part—that's why we're starting in the middle of our story instead of the beginning. We can come back and work this scene over later, after we're in the groove. We're saving the beginning scenes for when we've got the wind up and are moving like greased lightning again, that magnificent soaring feeling of being a *writer*.

Scene after scene after scene. *Writing*.

Now do this for a really...long...time.

Staying in Motion

Do it.

Resting When Necessary

Do this, too. We'll get up and go downstairs at the end of each day of work. Hug our shnookums. Sit on the back porch listening to the frogs in the sunset. Rub our bare feet in the dirt. Scrub our scalp.

Think about how lucky we are to be alive.

We'll wake up the next morning thinking about that next scene we're going to write that day.

Rewriting Out of Chronology

We can go ahead and leap around in the manuscript. If we get the urge to write for a long time, we can always blast through a whole series of scenes that have yet to be written. If we're feeling a bit skittish and unfocused, we can fill in the gaps between scenes we've already written or migrated over from our first draft.

We'll try not to go back to the beginning and write a fresh Hook until we've gotten most of Conflict #1 and maybe Conflict #2 finished—even the Faux Resolution. Conflict #3 is second only to the Hook in importance, and the Hook is second only to the Climax.

We'll write our most powerful scenes when we feel really on *fire*. We want our skills to be at their most scintillating when we write those.

Taking Notes

And as we write, we always take lots of notes. We'll keep a notebook open by our side and pause to jot down significant bits at the ends of scenes. We'll pause in the middle of scenes if we think we'll forget by the end, but we'll do our best not to interrupt the flow. We're in the writing part of the brain.

Think of new scenes. New ideas! Our brains are frothing cauldrons of creativity! Write those new scenes. *Write.*

A Word of Warning about Resolution

But whatever we do, *we won't write our Resolution.*

I don't care whether or not we wrote one for our first draft Sometimes we have to write one to get it out of our system. But after that. . .let it lie.

Focusing on our Resolution now will diffuse our energy and congest the flow of the narrative. We're not going to save these characters from their doom right now. We're not going to resolve their nightmare. We're going to abandon them to their fate, and we're going to make that the worst possible fate we have in us.

We're going to make their nightmare so damn gorgeous even *they* can't think about anything else.

Remember the Tao of theme.

Chapter 29

Spiraling Up the Helix
Multiple drafts

And will that draft be the final draft?

I mean, really—how many drafts could it *possibly* take?

This is the hollow, diabolical chorus of laughter from every serious writer who ever has come before us on this planet, living or dead. That burst of laughter's not fading away, either. It's getting louder and more cacophonic, a swelling orchestra of demented shouts and mocking hee-hawing and shrieks, until it degenerates into the deafening noise of Original Chaos, exactly how the universe sounded just before the Big Bang.

I'm sorry. I don't make them do that. They just launch into it every time someone asks that question.

The answer, of course, is: *far more drafts than we can ever imagine.*

But for your convenience and out of the sheer kindness of my heart, I'm going to narrow that number down to five. Five *complete* drafts.

First Draft

The first draft is for the writer. *Zippety doo-dah!* We're having *some* kind of a good time!

We can pants if it's absolutely necessary. I pantsed five novels before I got wise, and now I plot mine out ahead of time. But I still write that first draft just for me.

Some of the lines that come out of me as though by osmosis — *oh,* that's the reason I do this work.

Second Draft

The middle drafts are for the characters. They have a story. We may or may not know what that story is. But it's our job to find out and then tell it.

So we work our way through our protagonist's real character arc, and we use that to develop their real narrative arc. We design a new draft with all the scenes we're keeping and the scenes we're discarding and the scenes we have yet to write.

And we write that second draft, making a point of cleaning up our grammar and spelling and punctuation as we do so, because if we don't we're going to have one *heck* of a time reading it objectively later to determine whether or not it's beginning to sound plausible. Remember that our goal with each successive draft is to be progressing from amateur to professional. If we refuse to improve, we're just spinning our wheels.

We finish that second draft, by which time we're probably truly and heartily finished with this whole thing. It must be done, *mustn't* it? It's just like when your baby first learns to communicate with gestures, before they learn to speak. That fundamental act of communication is the big hurdle, isn't it? Isn't the rest of it — all that learning to talk and study and take college exams and everything — kind of anti-climactic once they've gotten the gist of it?

We know any small, trivial errors we might have left in this draft will be practically invisible in the glare of genius with which the rest is so thoroughly infused.

So we put it in a drawer to go cold. And we go away for awhile.

Third Draft

This is a baffling draft. This is where we pull that manuscript out of the drawer some months (or years) later and read it through.

It's not *almost done*. Good grief. It's barely *started*.

I can't teach you how to keep this from happening, but I can promise that the longer we let it go cold, the less painful this moment is.

If we let it go cold for a really long time—six months, people, a year—we'll have forgotten by then how certain we were when we put it away in that drawer that it was simply the *living end*. We'll have developed other babies that we've been working on in the meantime. We'll be, frankly, rather taken aback by how good it is when we come across lines, paragraphs, whole scenes we've forgotten we wrote. We're writers! This is so thrilling to read! *In spite* of how little we knew about the craft way, way back in the Dark Ages when we wrote it.

Hey, there's some real gold in here. This might be salvageable!

So we do another round with character arc and narrative arc, looking specifically for holes in the logic and great, galumphing windows onto whole vistas we were blind to before. We heave a rather impatient sigh and Copy Edit it with a red pen, perhaps hoping to shame our writerly selves out of the habit of confusing 'your' and 'you're' and jumping tenses like we're playing leapfrog.

We create a whole new batch of fresh, untouched documents into which we migrate the scenes we want to keep (more than last time—yippee!) and outline the ones we're chomping at the bit to write.

And again, we *write*. Scene after scene after scene. Sinking into that fictional world we left behind so long ago. Looking around at it with unexpected lucidity, with a sensitivity to telling detail and significant action and witty dialog we never had for this story in its early incarnations.

And we fall in love all over again. We'll have those great scenes we wrote without knowing we were writing them so well to spur us on. We're developing our skills—we're *writers*.

Then, with much greater equanimity than last time, we'll put it away again.

We have those other babies calling out to us.

Nth Draft

This draft is like the open-walls phase of building a house, when we've got a house framed up and we've got a lot of electric wires and plumbing and insulation and unidentifiable stuff that we don't even know what it is. All we know is that all that stuff has to go into our walls before we can seal them up permanently.

This draft takes for-freaking-*ever*.

And it breaks our heart while it does it. This is the Draft of Despair.

The last time we took this manuscript out of cold storage, we were both shocked and pleased, expecting both much more and much less than what we found.

But this draft doesn't seem to have changed *at all*.

Why hasn't anything happened to it? Wasn't there some kind of alchemy that was supposed to alter its basic molecular structure while we weren't looking? Weren't there things we were supposed to have forgotten, things we weren't supposed to have seen before? Some of our improvements have worked, yes, but some of them must be restored to the way they were in the first place. Even then this story is completely predictable. These characters are *weak*!

There's a lot of crying during the first part of this draft. This is the draft that drives even the most professional writers to drink.

Later we pull ourselves together (possibly out from under our beds) and do some reading up on craft in our favorite books on writing. We ask a writer friend to show us their working manuscript—"Not for critiquing. I'll just give you a general thumbs-up." So they do, and we do, and we don't tell them they've given us a fresh lease on life when we see *nobody's* doing it the way we know in our heart of hearts it truly ought to be done.

We take a lot of notes based on the reading we're doing, then we go into this draft and ruthlessly toss all the stuff we've been saving from draft to draft that we sort of knew shouldn't be there but were awfully proud of. We repair past improvements that didn't work.

We spend some time staring at the chaotic shambles of what was once upon a time so vivid and meaningful and true.

And then we go get an opinion from an independent editor.

Final Draft

The final draft is for the reader.

And I am sorry. I truly wish I could tell you that we can do this draft without professional help. But with the industry in the condition it's in, the increasingly-rigid guidelines for publication and growing dependence upon famous names, the mushrooming number of aspiring writers competing with us for those dwindling precious spots on agents' and publishers' calendars, the cramming of bookstore shelves as POD brings back into eternal print all the lost treasures of literature and a whole industry blooms around trading on the well-known names of the dead, plus the intense flood of self-publishing, plus now the option of ebooks—it's either professional help or a *really, really long apprenticeship*. Say, thirty years.

I strongly recommend taking advantage of the guidance of an independent editor, which is available to us now for the first time in the history of aspiring writers.

And when we finally do take it we're on our way, learning what we need to do with this story and how to do it the way we've always dreamed. We're being encouraged and challenged, compassionately supported and unsentimentally prodded, treated like a professional writer by this editor we've chosen who works with other writers to make beautiful and true their unfinished or even failed manuscripts *all the time*.

We're writers.

Writers who love their stories.

So we learn to accept the specific elements of this particular story. (Originally we wanted it to have *everything*, but now we know there are some things that will have to go in our next book, the one already popping and fizzing in the back of our brain.)

We're prepared to use the skills we're developing to offer our reader the very best version of this one story we can produce, knowing it's no longer about falling into a great story by luck or winning the rich-&-famous lottery or stumbling inadvertently upon a genius talent we always suspected in our soul but never had proof of before.

There's simply someone we will never meet out there in the world who doesn't know how to do this work and yet desperately needs help understanding their life. This one life they get. And we *do* know how to do this work. We've spent a long, dedicated time apprenticing ourselves to it, and now we're being mentored on a professional level.

This particular story can help that person. We can give that anonymous sufferer what they need—hope, validation, some greater awareness of the world, of paradoxical meaning—to make their life feel *real*.

And it turns out nothing else matters, after all.

Chapter 30

Going Beyond the Beyond

The far side of Hell

I don't like horror movies—even squashed bugs gross me out—but I *love* the movie *Flatliners*. I love that concept of what's beyond the beyond.

You know how it is whenever we start a story, how we're flames alight, burning up everything around us, the very atoms of the air fuel for our creation? Our characters walk among mortals like creatures from a visionary universe. They live and breathe, crack wise, laugh, put a tender hands on our arm. They learn bad news, and our eyes fill. When their hearts break, we're sobbing as we type. Just sitting around the kitchen table with them all morning talking gossip as the sun crosses the window is as fulfilling as human contact can ever be. Everything we never get from real life is here, in these manuscript pages, waiting for us to wake up every day and join them again.

Fiction is our way of creating a tribe for ourselves.

Then we've gotten it all down, and we're transforming it from our own personal tribe into, well, literature. The first part is about our needs. The rest is about everyone else's. Now we're creating a plot, an adventure for these characters, and we're using what we know about them to tell how they would act in any given situation, to show how they get themselves from one pickle into another, what facility they have for disaster.

We don't want to do dreadful things to them. But there is that reader out there. And the reader wants our characters to help them understand the turmoil of real life.

So we do that part, too. Then we go into revision. Because we've had to combine these agendas—ours, our characters', and the reader's—and naturally there are some glitches. This takes innumerable passes. At first we're drunk on the reality. Then we're drunk on the power of fiction to *speak*. Then we're drunk on the sheer potential for transforming this world that has meant so much to us into something that could mean so much to a complete stranger, simply through the artifice of language and fictional tools. It happens. It really does! We've all read books of a beauty to take the breath away. And we too can be among those who walk with our feet in the stars.

Finally we wake up one morning and go to our desk and pick up the pages...and something snaps inside. And we realize we're never going to get those words to transform.

Never.

Our reach has exceeded our grasp.

By about *five light-years*.

So here we sit with our faces lying sideways on the desk, feeling the tears trickle ever-so-slowly down to the bridge of our nose, across it, and drop with the most delicate little irritating mosquito-touch from our nose to the desk under our cheek. Our neck hurts, but it doesn't matter.

Nothing will ever matter again.

This is the point, in *Flatliners*, in which we have medically anesthetized ourselves to the point of death and just beyond, and we discover—much to our surprise—that the beyond is Hell.

And yet it seemed like such a good idea at the time!

Now, I am not here to act as our medical-student cohorts pulling us back from the anesthesia. I am not our pals reeling us in, waking us from the nightmare, patting everyone jovially on the back, and helping us off the table. "You're not really dead. That didn't really happen. *Psyche!*" Those are not the words coming out of my mouth.

Because I know something about that. I know when someone does that, *Hell follows us home.*

And then we are well and truly haunted. The glaring errors remain and get worse. The stumbling blocks trip us up more and more, throwing us headfirst into the muck and mire faster and more heartlessly every time we attempt that impossible task of transformation. Peer critiques, if we get them, become more random and less predictable. No one can agree on what's going wrong!

We might stick with it because the hype about Becoming a Writer is so powerful and omnipresent out there, and besides now all our friends are Becoming Writers too. Or because we're stubborn cusses and don't know when we're beat. Or because we have a story we desperately want to tell. Or simply because we've always looked up to our favorite authors, all our life, and dreamed with our heart in our throat of the day we would join their ranks.

But the secret pain is crippling. And it is countered only by the numbness of turning ourselves into donkeys plodding in joyless drudgery after that coveted carrot.

No.

I am here to do the opposite: to push us through—because on the other side of Hell is *craft*.

And we can't get there by backing out. We must dive forward into the agony—sitting there with our face lying sideways on the desk—and discover within it every reason writing is an *inanely* bad idea.

Tackle a task we only know vaguely through the second-hand results of someone else's lifelong efforts? Tackle it with the wild-eyed hope that, although it takes professional writers their entire lives to polish their skills, years to produce a single novel, and the nearly-unlimited assistance of publishing professionals they pretty much lucked into, it will take us a matter of months because, after all, didn't Faulkner write *As I Lay Dying* in six weeks? Tackle it with the idea of supporting ourselves, even though the greats almost universally died penniless and unknown? Tackle it with minimal training and experience, barely a smidgen of comprehension, a whole lot of optimism, and the encouragement of people who stand to gain financially by our ambitions? Tackle it with nothing but our bare hands?

We will lie there and sob. Gnash our teeth. This is how we learn to be us.

And when we are done, we will know something about life we didn't know before. We will know how to survive. We will have gone *beyond* the beyond into the ephemeral, multi-faceted, tactile alternate reality of endless potential we knew was there—we wanted so badly to believe in—all along.

And then we'll have something to write about.

Conclusion

Riding Out the Winter of Our Discontent

The writing life

Oh, what a summer it's been—nearly endless overcast and rain last spring until almost the Summer Solstice, and then suddenly one weekend of hot, baking, Augustine days. My son reported cheerfully that it was 90 degrees in the shade. I sat under my holey old umbrella in the weedy meadow and sfanned myself with a paperback like Blanche duBois (dependent, in this case, upon the kindness of the brilliant mystery writer Ngaio Marsh).

This is the writing life.

We get into it for the glory of the page. It's exactly like the day summer arrives—there's something tangible in the air, something that makes us sit up and smell the wind, turn to the horizon and say to ourselves, "I'd forgotten. The reason I'm alive."

People come to us in our daydreams, and they want to tell us what's happened to them, where they've been, what they saw there, whom they met, what they said to each other. They're intensely striking personalities. We take one look at them, and we're already a little in love. So we're willing to listen. We're even, as Anne Lamott says, willing to transcribe it all.

We're so enthralled we can't imagine this story ever ending.

At the same time, the world is chock full to the eyeballs these days with the push to publish. We'd have to be more than oblivious not to have noticed—we'd have to be *dead*. So as soon as we meet these characters and agree to be their scribe, we feel the heavy gravitational pull of publication dragging at our neck.

The rains are back. They beat and beat and beat at our windows, streaming down the glass and obscuring our vision. They make mud of our yard so every time we leave the house we worry about slipping and breaking our neck. They flatten the blossoms that were beginning to appear, tear them off the bushes and turn them to mush, bring up the weeds before we can get outside to pull them, rot our back steps, fill our gutters with wet leaves until water overflows deathly cold on our head and—if we're really out of luck—defaces our ceilings with ominous, creeping brown stains.

We struggle and struggle to fight off the unseasonable rains, but they're washing us away.

And then one day we wake up, and the power's out, so we can't go online to check our email or Twitter or read blog posts on writing or dither around lending credibility as a writer to and accepting it from people we don't know, puffing each other's egos with talk of wordcounts and writerly preoccupation, with self-marketing and PR and query letters, patting each other on the back for being writers.

We're stranded! There's nothing for us to do now...except write.

We gird our loins. We haul a dusty old typewriter out of the back of the closet and brush it off or, if we don't have one, pick up a pen. We don't keep notebooks in the house anymore, but we do have paper bags.

We look at the pen in one hand and the paper bag in the other.

This is *ridiculous*.

But we're writers. So we sit down at the kitchen table. We take a deep breath. And we begin to write.

To write and write and write...

And when we look up hours later, we're sitting in a hot, glorious, weedy meadow under a holey old umbrella. Children are shouting with laughter and spraying the hose in the distance. Bees hang from the edges of vivid orange poppies near our knees, and a silky, half-grown black cat steps fastidiously through the grass in our direction. The smell of earth rises between our feet, the smell of dry-rot rises from the huge stump in which our umbrella stands, the smell of grass seed ripening rises into the white, white sun.

Ngaio Marsh's brilliant Chief Detective-Inspector Alleyn leans over and explains drily, in the most charming patter possible, exactly what hangs in the balance—and then asks inexplicably if we like party metaphors.

The world is brilliant with detail and charisma and utterly mysterious significance.

We're alive! Alive. This is how it feels to *be alive*.

Index

A

addiction 67, 140
addictive 71
Alcott
   Beth 95
   Bronson 93, 94
   Louisa May ....
         .... 93, 94, 95, 96, 142
Alice Through the Looking-Glass 108
Anderson, Edward ....
         .... 164, 187, 188
Anna Karenina . 186, 241, 250
Arden, Eve 69
argyle socks 36
Art & Craft of Fiction: A Practitioner's Manual, The
         .... 76, 83, 159
As I Lay Dying 300
"Aspern Papers, The" 59, 104, 250
Aunt Julia and the Scriptwriter 22
Austen, Jane .. 54, 59, 71, 185

B

Baby Jesus Pawn Shop 123
Balzac, Honoré de 34
Barnum & Bailey 17
Bartlett, Craig 35
beans, full of 69
believable .. 23, 113, 143, 144
Bellow, Saul 103, 143
Bence, Amelia 49
Bird by Bird 122
birdcages 79
Bogart, Humphrey ....
         .... 133, 134, 137
Bond, James 108
Bowen, Elizabeth 103
Bowles, Paul 73
Bradbury, Ray ....
      ..... 167, 187, 188, 204, 211
Bronte
   Branwell 95
   Charlotte 54, 77
   Emily ... 54, 55, 87, 95, 146
Brothers Karamozov, The .. 50, 250

Index

C

Cain, James M. 146, 169, 171, 172, 173, 187, 188
calligraphy...................... 275
carbon-freeze................... 70
Castle of Otranto, The 178, 179, 187, 188, 189, 191, 193, 194, 195, 196, 197, 199, 200, 201, 204, 205, 207, 209, 210, 212, 214, 216, 217, 220, 221, 223, 224, 226, 227, 228, 230, 231, 233, 250
Castle, The 263, 264, 265
cause-&-effect......................
...27, 31, 33, 58, 67, 78, 97, 99, 100, 101, 102, 136, 137, 171, 177, 267
Cervantes, Miguel de ... 235
chaise longue................. 126
Chandler, Raymond 163
character 31
   one-dimensional........ 114
   sympathetic..38, 113, 116
   three-dimensional ....
   ....78, 115
   two-dimensional....... 114
   unsympathetic 113
character arc..39, 40, 41, 42, 45, 46, 58, 267, 273, 274, 275, 276, 277, 281, 282, 290, 291

Chinese New Year 65
choice 124, 130, 133, 134, 135, 136, 137, 145, 243, 274, 275
Christie, Agatha............. 163
Christmas Carol, A...... 97, 99
claymation....................... 35
Closed Mondays 35
coincidence.............136, 220
Colantoni, Enrico............ 51
Collins, Wilkie................. 54
Color Kittens, The 71
Community of Writers at Squaw Valley 121
Compton-Burnett, Ivy ... 55, 87
conflict
   external......................... 71
   internal ....
   ... 28, 41, 42, 67, 68, 69, 71, 115, 123, 127, 141, 272
confusion 143, 144
Conrad, Joseph.............. 249
constellations................... 85
contrast 124
cosmology 40
Cousin Rosamund trilogy.*see Fountain Overflows, The*
Crime and Punishment....... 51
critters 78
Croesus 236

306

crux of the matter, the .. 242
Czechoslovakia 258, 264

D

Dark Passage 133, 145, 250
Day at the Circus, A 69
Delta Wedding 55
"Deluge at Norderney,
 The" ... 182, 187, 189, 190,
 191, 193, 194, 195, 196,
 197, 199, 200, 201, 204,
 205, 207, 209, 210, 212,
 214, 216, 218, 220, 221,
 223, 224, 226, 227, 228,
 230, 231, 233, 250
Dermout, Maria 149, 163
deus ex machina 98
Developmental
 Demonstration 129
Dickens, Charles 99
Dinesen, Isak . 181, 182, 187,
 189, 195, 233
Dinosaur Train 35
Dolce 140, 146, 250
domino 41, 42
Don Quixote 55, 57
*Don't Crush That Dwarf,
 Hand Me the Pliers* 36
Dostoevsky, Fyodor. 50, 51,
 116, 185
duBois, Blanche 301
ducks, charming 124

Duke Kahuna, the 21
"Dwarf, The" .167, 187, 188,
 189, 190, 192, 194, 195,
 196, 197, 198, 200, 201,
 204, 206, 208, 209, 211,
 212, 213, 216, 217, 220,
 221, 222, 224, 225, 227,
 229, 231, 232, 250

E

Earnshaw, Catherine 115
Ecuador 83
#editingchat 129
editor 62, 294
 acquisitions 163, 164
 independent 293, 294
 newspaper 136
Emerson, Ralph Waldo ... 93
Emma 71, 185, 240
empathy 131, 240
End of the Affair, The 52
entirety of our imaginary
 worlds, the 86
epiphany ....
 .... 46, 85, 89, 90, 132, 143,
 185, 207, 228, 230, 233,
 241, 259, 279
eraser 64
exercises 61, 64

F

Fair Play 79
fairytales 55

307

Index

faith 90
falls down
   house with no
      supporting walls 63
fantasy 36, 37, 58, 167
Faulkner, William 53, 55, 300
Favorita, La 84
fiction 35
   great, vast luxury of . 131
Field, Syd 153
Firesign Theater 36
Flatliners 297, 299
Fleming, Ian 108
Ford, Harrison 117
Fountain Overflows, The ....
      .... 100, 250, 251
Frankenstein 55
funny stuff, knock it off ......
      109

G

Galaxy Quest 51, 57
Galaxy Song, The 48
Gardiner, Bob 35
Gardner, Erle Stanley ... 163
genre 71
   adventure 57
   buddy 54, 55
   family drama 55
   fantasy 61, 72, 98, 247
   ghost story 97, 98, 242

gothic 178, 187
horror 54, 72, 178, 187
literary 187
mystery ....
   ... 51, 54, 55, 72, 78, 79, 178, 301
paranormal 178, 187
romance 53, 54, 56, 73
series 61
thriller 54, 72, 169, 178, 187
Gibson, William 56
"Gold Bug" 79
Golden Gate Bridge 135
gong, brass 76, 80
good time, having one 80
Goodis, David ....
   .... 133, 135, 136, 145
Gordian Knot 42
Gormenghast 37, 38, 265
granularity 40
Greene, Graham 52
Grey, Zane 172, 173, 177, 187, 188
Groan, Fuschia 38

H

hacienda 83
head-hunters 150, 151
Heart of Darkness 249, 250
Heathcliff 115, 116
Heinlein, Robert A 87

Henderson the Rain King 103, 143, 144, 250
highlighted wrinkles, wonderful 84
Hillary Waugh's Guide to Mystery & Mystery Writing 79
hobbit's eleventy-first birthday 65
hogwash, altruistic 142
holo
 gram 39
 graph 39
 -something 40
holographic structure .. 153, 159
Homer 236
hoovering 71
Hosseini, Khaled 23
Hotel Splendid 47
Human Comedy, The 34

I

Idiot, The 185, 239, 250
If It's Tuesday, This Must Be Belgium 257
images, stylized 85, 90
imperatives 40
inciting incident 99, 102
inevitable . 24, 33, 42, 43, 80, 81, 101, 107, 132, 178, 248, 252, 264
interminable, all but 88

Irving, Washington 186
itsy-bitsy little facial features 84, 86

J

James, Henry 59, 100, 104
Jane Eyre 77

K

Kafka, Franz ... 263, 264, 265
King, Stephen 29, 163
Kite Runner, The 23
knickers 76

L

Lamott, Anne 122, 302
Last September, The 103
layering 141
"Legend of Sleepy Hollow, The" 186, 242
Life and Hard Times, My 55
link 76, 152
 between two disparate things 76
Little Women 93, 95, 250
Llosa, Mario Vargas 22
logic 98, 99, 100, 101, 102, 108, 284, 291
logo 83
Lord Byron 126
love 144

Index

Love in the Time of Cholera 22, 24
Luisardo, Tito 49

M

magic 80, 90
   wand 36
Marquez, Gabriel Garcia ....
   ....21, 22, 24
Marsh, Ngaio 301, 303
Marx, Groucho 69
McKee, Robert................. 99
Meaning of Life, The.......... 48
Mexican Independence .. 65
Michelangelo's David... 122
Middle Grade (MG)...67, 68
milemarker 88
mistakes 117, 135, 142
Modern Magic: Five Stories
   95
Modern Mephistopheles, and A Whisper in the Dark, A
   95
Moll Flanders 55, 57
momentum 132
Monty Python 48
motivation 136, 141, 143,
   193, 248, 250
"Murders in the Rue
   Morgue, The" 79
Mysteries of Udolpho, The. 58
"Mystery of Marie Roget,
   The" 79

N

narrative arc ..39, 41, 42, 45,
   46, 267, 278, 281, 282,
   283, 290, 291
Naylor family, the 103
Nemirovsky, Irene ....
   ....140, 145
Neuromancer 56
Nicholson, Harold 125

O

O'Connor, Flannery .31, 254
October Country, The 167
"107 Things You Should
   Know About Being a
   Published Author" 29
*One Hundred Years of
   Solitude* 22
option paralysis 135
Orth, Lucia 123
ostrich feathers, violet 83

P

Pandora's Box 16
Panther Jack ...237, 238, 303
pants 78, 243, 290
paper bags 303
paradox in our souls,
   irreconcilable............... 42
parents' faces, looks on .. 40
participles 40
Peake, Mervyn ...37, 38, 265

pièce de résistance 84, 89
plot 31
pluperfect 40
Poe, Edgar Allan 54, 79
Polo, Marco 57, 58
Portland 35, 61
Postman Always Rings Twice, The ... 146, 169, 172, 187, 188, 189, 190, 192, 194, 195, 196, 197, 198, 200, 201, 204, 205, 206, 208, 210, 211, 212, 214, 216, 217, 220, 221, 222, 224, 225, 227, 229, 231, 232, 250
Prague 258, 263, 264
premise .. 28, 86, 97, 99, 102, 172, 185, 186, 237, 238, 243, 245, 252, 274, 275, 276
Pride and Prejudice 59
proa 151, 152
prodromal labor 285
Proust, Marcel 119
publication ... 30, 50, 53, 294, 302
pulp .... *See* vintage
"Purloined Letter, The" .. 79
push-pull 116, 134, 138

Q

quantum mechanics 40

Queen, Ellery 79
quest 47, 50, 51, 57, 264
  external 48, 57, 58
  internal 48, 58

R

Radcliffe, Mrs. 58, 178
railroad tracks 72
realism 35
reality ....
  ...... 27, 108, 132, 144, 230, 298, 300
Redonnet, Marie 47
relationship 47, 50
Remembrance of Things Past 119
retro-design 274
Revisionland 268
Rhys, Jean 54, 249
rhythm, primal 161
Rickman, Alan 51
Riders of the Purple Sage 172, 187, 188, 189, 191, 192, 194, 195, 196, 197, 198, 200, 201, 204, 205, 207, 208, 210, 212, 214, 216, 217, 220, 221, 223, 224, 225, 227, 228, 229, 231, 232, 250
Rockwell, Sam 51
rodents, noises coming out of 75

Index

Romeo & Juliet 185, 239, 250
Rover 257

S

Sackville-West, Vita 125
San Francisco 21, 61, 80, 135, 137, 169
Sarris 52
Saturday Night Live 52
Science & Entertainment Exchange 26, 27
science fiction 26, 27, 36, 52, 55, 56, 167
scones, not invented 77
Screenplay 153
Scrooge 97
SETI 25
Seuss, Dr. 188
Seven Samurai, The 55
Shakespeare, William .. 185, 236
Shalhoub, Tony 51
Shatner, William 52
Shelley, Mary 55
ship, jump 88
shnookums 286
shocking 248
siblings, twenty-four 124
sleight-of-hand 80
soulful gaze 84
spice park 149

Star Trek 26, 51
Steinbeck, John 249
story 32
Stranger in a Strange Land ... 87
subject 39
Superhero, weeping 67
surrealism 35
survival ... 138, 144, 145, 146
worth it 138

T

Tao 46, 279, 287
Ten Thousand Things, The 149
Tess of the D'Urbervilles ... 78
Thieves Like Us, a romance 164, 187, 188, 189, 190, 192, 193, 195, 196, 198, 200, 204, 206, 208, 209, 211, 212, 213, 215, 217, 220, 222, 224, 225, 227, 229, 231, 232, 250
Thoreau, Henry David ... 93
"Thou Art The Man" 79
Thurber, James 55
tiger eats them 102
To the Lighthouse 249
Tolstoy, Leo 186
Tom Jones 55, 57
tongues, lolling 103
Tortilla Flat 249

Transcendentalists 93
truth . 24, 27, 28, 70, 76, 140, 151, 182, 197
"Turn of the Screw, The"
.... 100

U

underbelly
    dark, disturbing 95
    iridescent 280
unknowable, the 108
unsayable, the 108

V

values 42, 141, 142, 143
Van Dyke, Dick 37
verb 39
vintage .... 162, 163, *See* pulp
Vinton, Will 35
Violent Bear It Away, The
    .... 103, 250, 254
visceral response 76

W

Waiting for the Electrician or Someone Like Him 36
Walpole, Horace 54, 178, 179, 180, 181, 187, 188, 189

Waugh, Hillary 79
weird 37, 84, 88, 284
Welty, Eudora 55
West, Rebecca ... 55, 61, 100, 251, 252
whimper 67, 184, 236
whining 97
White King, the 108, 109, 279
whole tantalizing pie, the ...
.... 80
Wide Sargasso Sea 249
Williams, Tennessee 301
Witness Protection
    Program 125
Woolf, Virginia 249
Wooster, Bertie 236
work habits 15
Wuthering Heights ... 87, 146, 250

Y

Young Adult (YA) 247

Z

zen 39
zippety doo-dah! 289

Made in the USA
Lexington, KY
09 April 2013